Needless Hunger

Voices from a Bangladesh Village

Betsy Hartmann & James Boyce

FOOD FIRST BOOKS
OAKLAND, CALIFORNIA

FRONT COVER DESIGN BY KERRY TREMAIN

COVER PHOTO BY HARTMANN/BOYCE

BOOK DESIGN BY BARBARA GARZA

Library of Congress Cataloging-in-Publication Data
Hartmann, Betsy
Needless Hunger: voices from a Bangladesh village/
Betsy Hartmann, James K. Boyce
p. cm.
Includes bibliography.
ISBN 0-935028-03-X
1. Food supply—Bangladesh. 2. Hunger. 3. Agriculture—Bangladesh. 4. Bangladesh—Rural conditions. I. Boyce, James K., joint author. II. Institute for Food and Development Policy.

HD9016.B352H37
338,195492 – dc19 80-142853
CIP

Eleventh Printing

Food First Books are distributed by: CDS; (800) 343-4499

Map: Formerly East Pakistan, Bangladesh was founded in 1971 following the Bengali revolt against Pakistan. Officially known as Gana Prajatantri Bangladesh (People's Republic of Bangladesh) and lying in the delta of the Ganges and Brahmaputra rivers, Bangladesh is 55,126 square miles (142,776 square kilometers) in area, approximately the size of Wisconsin. Bangladesh is the fourth largest agricultural society in the world; ninety percent of its 83 million people are rural, and eighty percent depend directly upon agriculture as a livelihood. According to the Food and Agriculture Organization of the United Nations, "Bangladesh is possibly the richest country in the world as far as inland fishery resources are concerned."

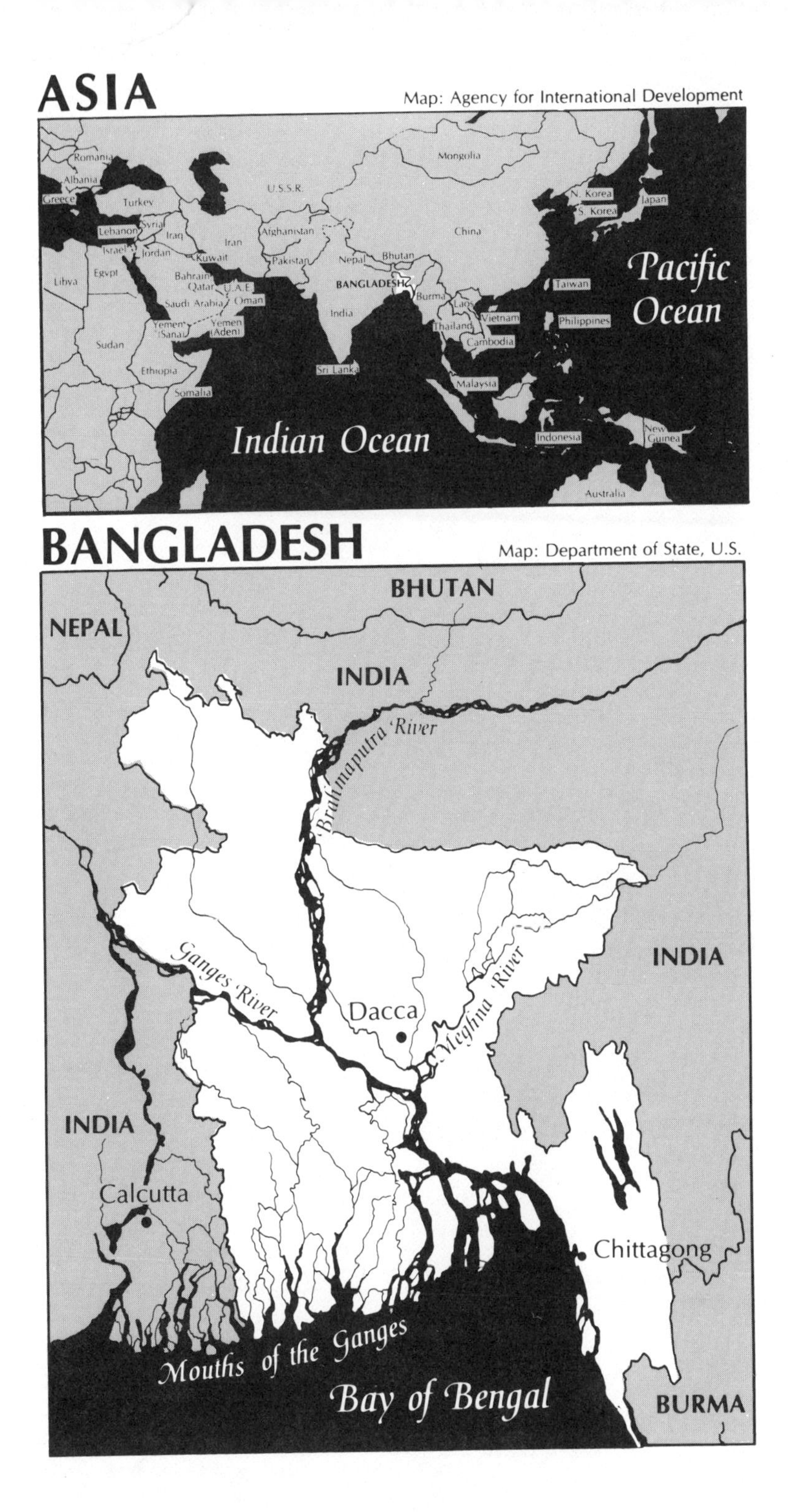
ASIA
Map: Agency for International Development
Romania
Albania
Greece
Turkey
U.S.S.R.
Mongolia
N. Korea
S. Korea
Japan
Syria
Lebanon
Iraq
Iran
Afghanistan
China
Israel
Jordan
Kuwait
Pakistan
Nepal
Bhutan
Libya
Egypt
Bahrain
Qatar
U.A.E.
BANGLADESH
Taiwan
Pacific Ocean
Saudi Arabia
Oman
Burma
Laos
India
Yemen (Sanai)
Yemen (Aden)
Vietnam
Philippines
Thailand
Sudan
Cambodia
Ethiopia
Sri Lanka
Somalia
Malaysia
Indian Ocean
Indonesia
New Guinea
Australia
BANGLADESH
Map: Department of State, U.S.
BHUTAN
NEPAL
INDIA
Brahmaputra River
INDIA
Ganges River
Dacca
Meghna River
INDIA
Calcutta
Chittagong
Mouths of the Ganges
Bay of Bengal
BURMA

Contents

Many who read *Food First: Beyond the Myth of Scarcity* find among its most shocking revelations the fact that Bangladesh isn't a hopeless basketcase: there are indeed enough resources in that country to provide for all. The media-generated image of an entire people condemned to perpetual hunger is now being challenged. The truth is more hopeful, if paradoxical: despite its current low productivity, Bangladesh may already produce enough grain for all its people. Moreover, it has barely tapped its agricultural potential — among the greatest in the world.

Many people want to learn more about Bangladesh, for they sense, as we do, that Bangladesh provides lessons with implications well beyond its national scope. If hunger is needless in this foremost "basketcase," it is indeed needless in every other country in the world.

Here in *Needless Hunger*, Betsy Hartmann and James Boyce share their own direct experiences and lessons drawn from the villages of Bangladesh. Hartmann and Boyce, Bengali-speaking Americans and Fellows of the Institute for Food and Development Policy, spent two years (1974-1976) living in Bangladesh and nine months in one typical rural village. Their growing familiarity with the daily struggles and conflicts within the village allowed them to cut through the seeming irrationality of hunger to find its political and economic roots. The authors describe how the few have gained effective control over productive resources, leading to both the underuse and misuse of these resources. We learn of the perceptions, fears and frustrations of those who strain to survive in rural Bangladesh against the weight of unjust social and economic structure.

But the authors do not only present us with a microscopic view of Bangladesh society. They describe in concise terms how the local hierarchy is supported at the national level. Indeed, Hartmann and Boyce demonstrate how we in the West are directly linked to the very forces that generate hunger in Bangladesh. The United States, Canada, Great Britain, Norway, Sweden, Holland, Saudi Arabia, Japan, France, Germany, etc., all have large "development assistance" programs in Bangladesh. These programs — together with those of the multilateral agencies like the U. N. 's World Food Program and the World Bank — now total well over $1 billion a year. Hartmann and Boyce show from their own on-site investigations that such aid often undermines the very people with whom we would most wish to ally ourselves — the hungry and impoverished. Similarly, the authors help us understand that no matter how good our government's intentions, the massive food aid we are told is for the hungry in fact ends up feeding and enriching a privileged minority.

But *Needless Hunger* is not a story without hope. Hartmann and Boyce reveal the strength and potential of the Bangladesh people. They argue that social reconstruction could bring genuine economic progress for all. And they show that there is a way that we in the West can help: we can work to remove the obstacles to social change being built by forces of intervention which shore up the hunger status-quo.

The global analysis of our book *Food First* is vividly captured here in a single country — in a single village.

Frances Moore Lappe´
Joseph Collins

Bangladesh lies in the delta of three great rivers. *Photo by Hartmann/Boyce.*

1. The Paradox

In U.S. news media Bangladesh is usually portrayed as an "international basketcase," a bleak, desolate scene of hunger and despair. But when we arrived in Bangladesh in August 1974 we found a lush, green, fertile land. From the windows of buses and the decks of ferry boats, we looked over a landscape of natural abundance, everywhere shaped by the hands of men. Rice paddies carpeted the earth, and gigantic squash vines climbed over the roofs of the bamboo village houses. The rich soil, plentiful water and hot, humid climate made us feel as if we had entered a natural greenhouse.

As the autumn days grew clear and cool and the rice ripened in the fields, we saw why the Bengalis in song and verse call their land "golden Bengal." But that autumn we also came face to face with the extreme poverty for which Bangladesh has become so famous. When the price of rice soared in the lean season before the harvest, we witnessed the terrible spectacle of people dying in the streets of Dacca, the capital. Famine claimed thousands of lives throughout the country. The victims were Bangladesh's poorest people who could not afford to buy rice and had nothing left to sell.

As we tried to comprehend the contrast between the lush beauty of the land and the destitution of so many people, we sensed that we had entered a strange battleground. All around us silent struggles were being waged, struggles in which the losers met slow, bloodless deaths. In 1975 we spent nine months in the village of Katni, collecting material for a book on life in the Third World. There we learned more about the quiet violence which rages in Bangladesh.

Katni is a typical village. The majority of its 350 people are

---

"Bangladesh is rich enough in fertile land, water and natural gas for fertilizer not only to be self-sufficient in food, but a food exporter, even with its rapidly increasing population size."

---

poor: most families own less than two acres of land, and a quarter of the households are completely landless. The poorest often work for landlords in neighboring villages who own over 40 acres apiece. Four-fifths of the villagers are Muslims and one-fifth are Hindus. Except for two rickshaw pullers, all make their livings from agriculture.

To minimize the differences between ourselves and the

villagers, we lived in a small bamboo house, spoke Bengali and wore local clothing. By approaching the villagers as equals we were eventually able to win their trust. Jim spent most of his time talking with the men as they worked in the fields or went to the market, while Betsy spent most of her time talking with the women as they worked in and around their houses. The villagers taught us what it means to be hungry in a fertile land.

Golden Bengal

Bangladesh lies in the delta of three great rivers—the Brahmaputra, the Ganges and Meghna—which flow through it to empty into the Bay of Bengal (see map). The rivers and their countless tributaries meander over the flat land, constantly changing course, since most of the country lies less than 100 feet above sea level. The waters not only wash the land, they create it; their sediments have built the delta over the centuries. The alluvial soil deposited by the rivers is among the most fertile in the world.

Abundant rainfall and warm temperatures give Bangladesh an ideal climate for agriculture. Crops can be grown 12 months a year. The surface waters and vast underground aquifers give the country a tremendous potential for irrigation in the dry winter season. The rivers, ponds and rice paddies are alive with fish; according to a report of the United Nations Food and Agriculture Organization (FAO), "Bangladesh is possibly the richest country in the world as far as inland fishery resources are concerned."[1]

The country's dense human population bears testament to the land's fertility; historically the thick settlement of the delta, like that along the Nile River, was made possible by agricultural abundance. Today, with more than 80 million people, Bangladesh is the world's eighth most populous nation. Its population density is the highest of any country in the world except for Singapore and Hong Kong,[2] a fact which is all the more remarkable in light of the country's low level of urbanization. Nine out of 10 Bangladeshis live in villages, where most make their living from the land.

Bangladesh's soil may be rich, but its people are poor. The average annual income is less than $100 per person, the life expectancy only 47 years, and like all averages these overstate the well-being of the poorest.[3] A quarter of Bangladesh's children die before reaching the age of five.[4] Malnutrition claims many. Over half of Bangladesh's families consume less than the minimal calorie requirement, and 60 percent suffer from protein deficiencies.[5] Health care is poorly developed and concentrated in the urban areas. Less than a quarter of the population is literate.[6]

A United States Senate study notes that Bangladesh "is rich enough in fertile land, water, manpower and natural gas for fertilizer not only to be self-sufficient in food, but a food exporter, even with rapidly increasing population size."[7] But despite rich soil, ideal growing conditions and an abundant supply of labor, Bangladesh's agricultural yields are today among the lowest in the world. According to a World Bank document, "Present average yields of rice are about 1.2 metric tons per hectare, compared with 2.5 tons in Sri Lanka or 2.7 in Malaysia, which are climatically similar, or over 4 tons in Taiwan where labor inputs are greater."[8] Production has stagnated; today's yields are similar to those recorded 50 years ago.[9]

Why is a country with some of the world's most fertile land also the home of some of the world's hungriest people? A look at Bangladesh's history sheds some light on this paradox. The first Europeans to visit eastern Bengal, the region which is now Bangladesh, found a thriving industry and a prosperous agriculture. It was, in the optimistic words of one Englishman, "a wonderful land, whose richness and abundance neither war, pestilence nor oppression could destroy."[10] But by 1947, when the sun finally set on the British Empire in India, eastern Bengal had been reduced to an impoverished agricultural hinterland.

The British colonial rulers vested ownership of Bengal's land in *zamindars*. They lived well. *Agency for International Development photo.*

2. Riches to Rags

The Colonial Legacy

We in the industrialized nations often view development as a straightforward historical progression: poor countries are simply further behind on the path to development than rich ones. But this view ignores the fact that the destinies of nations have been linked, in ways which have often benefited one nation at the expense of another. In eastern Bengal, as in most of the third world, involvement with the West began with trade, and later gave way to direct political control by a colonial power. The legacy of Bangladesh's colonial history is a variation on a familiar theme: as the region became a supplier of agricultural raw materials to the world market, local industry withered and food production stagnated. The country not only did not develop, it actually underdeveloped.

European traders—first the Portuguese in the 16th century and later the Dutch, French and English—were lured to eastern Bengal by its legendary cotton textile industry, which ranked among the greatest industries in the world. Today, in a Dacca museum, one can see a specimen of the famous Dacca muslin, once prized in the imperial courts of Europe and Asia. A pale turban rests in a glass display case. Thirty feet long and three feet wide, the turban is so fine that it can be folded to fit inside an ordinary match box. The weavers of Dacca once produced this cloth on their handlooms, using thread spun from the cotton which grew along the banks of the nearby Meghna River. Today both the cotton and the weavers have disappeared. The variety of cotton plant adapted to the moist Bengali climate is extinct, and Bangladesh must import virtually all its cotton from abroad.

What happened to Bengal's cotton industry? After the British East India Company wrested control of Bengal from its Muslim rulers in 1757, the line between trade and outright plunder faded. In the words of an English merchant, "Various and innumerable are the methods of oppressing the poor weavers . . . such as by fines, imprisonments, floggings, forcing bonds from them, etc."[1] By means of "every conceivable form of roguery," the Company's merchants acquired the weaver's cloth for a fraction of its value.

Ironically, the profits from the lucrative trade in Bengali textiles helped to finance Britain's industrial revolution. As their own mechanized textile industry developed, the British eliminated competition from Bengali textiles through an elaborate network of restrictions and prohibitive duties. Not only were Indian textiles effectively shut out of the British market, but even within India taxes discriminated against local cloth.[2] The rapid decimation of local industry brought great hardship to the Bengali people. In 1835 the Governor-General of the East India Company reported to London, "The misery hardly finds a parallel in the history of commerce. The bones of the cotton weavers are bleaching the plains of India."[3]

The population of eastern Bengal's cities declined as the weavers were thrown back to the land. Sir Charles Trevelyan of the East India Company filed this report in 1840:

> The peculiar kind of silky cotton formerly grown in Bengal, from which the fine Dacca muslins used to be made, is hardly ever seen; the population of the town of Dacca has fallen from 150,000, to 30,000 or 40,000, and the jungle and malaria are fast encroaching upon the town . . . Dacca, which used to be the Manchester of India, has fallen off from a flourishing town to a very poor and small one.[4]

As Britain developed, Bengal underdeveloped.

With the decline of local industry, eastern Bengal assumed a new role as a supplier of agricultural raw materials. At first, using a contract labor system not far from slavery, European planters forced the Bengali peasants to grow indigo, the plant used to make blue dye. But in 1859 a great peasant revolt swept Bengal, and after this "indigo mutiny" the planters moved west to Bihar. Jute, the fiber used to make rope and burlap, soon became the region's main cash crop. By the turn of the century, eastern Bengal produced over half the world's jute, but under British rule not a single mill for its processing was ever built there. Instead, the raw jute was shipped for manufacture to Calcutta, the burgeoning metropolis of west Bengal, or exported to Britain and elsewhere.

The British not only promoted commercial agriculture, they also introduced a new system of land ownership to Bengal. Before their arrival, private ownership of agricultural land did not exist; land could not be bought and sold. Instead, the peasants had the right to till the soil, and *zamindars,* notables appointed by the Muslim rulers, had the right to collect taxes. Hoping to create a class of loyal supporters as well as to finance their own administration, the British in 1793 vested land ownership in the *zamindars,* who were henceforth required to pay a yearly tax to the British. In one stroke, land became private property which could be bought and sold. If a *zamindar* failed to pay his taxes, the state could auction his land.

The British set their original tax assessment so high that many estates were soon sold for arrears, and as a result, land rapidly changed hands from the old Muslim aristocracy to a rising class of Hindu merchants. In eastern Bengal, where the majority of peasants were Muslim, Hindu *zamindars* came to own three-quarters of the land. Conflicts between landlords and tenants began to take on a religious coloring.

The architects of the land settlement expected that the new landlords would devote their energies to improving their estates. But the *zamindars* found it far easier to collect rent than to invest in farming. Instead of agricultural entrepreneurs they became absentee landlords. Numerous intermediaries (sometimes as many as 50), each of whom subleased the land and took a share of the rent, arose between the *zamindars* and the actual tillers of the soil.[5] This led to exorbitant rents, which had a disastrous effect upon the peasants. Many were forced to borrow from moneylenders whose usurious interest rates further impoverished them. As early as 1832, a British inquiry commission concluded: "The settlement fashioned with great care and deliberation has to our painful knowledge subjected almost the whole of the lower classes to most grievous oppression."[6]

Little of the wealth extracted from the peasant producers by way of commercial agriculture, rent and land taxation was ever productively invested in Bengal. The budget of the colonial government clearly revealed the colonists' sense of priorities. Resources which could have financed development were instead devoted to subjugating the population. For example, in its 1935-36 budget, the Indian government devoted 703 million rupees to military services and the administration of justice, jails and the police. Another 527 million rupees were paid as interest, largely to British banks. Only 36 million were invested in agriculture and industry.[7]

Throughout their rule, the British also consciously exploited Hindu-Muslim antagonisms in a divide-and-rule strategy.[8] When they finally departed in 1947, Bengal was split along religious lines between the new independent nations of India and Pakistan. West Bengal, which was mainly Hindu and included Calcutta, went to India. Predominantly Muslim East Bengal became East Pakistan, joined in an awkward union with West Pakistan, a thousand miles away.

"In one stroke, land became private property which could be bought and sold."

Pakistan and the Birth of Bangladesh

With the creation of Pakistan many Hindu *zamindars* fled to India. In 1950 the oppressive zamindari system was legally abolished. Control of the land passed into the hands of a predominantly Muslim rural elite. Although the members of this new elite lived in the villages, they were reluctant to invest in agricultural production, preferring the easier profits to be made by moneylending and trade.

As East Pakistan, the east Bengal region did experience a

limited amount of industrial development. The first jute mills were finally built in the world's foremost jute-producing region. Growth remained stunted, however, by a new colonial relationship in which the West Pakistanis replaced the British. The majority of Pakistan's people lived in the eastern wing, yet westerners dominated the military and civil service. East Pakistan's jute was the main source of the nation's foreign exchange, but development expenditures were concentrated in West Pakistan. Incomes grew in the west but not in the east, and the widening disparities created political tensions between the two wings.

In 1971 these tensions culminated in civil war. The stage was set by the December 1970 national elections, when Sheikh Mujibur Rahman's Awami League won an overwhelming victory in East Pakistan on a platform of regional autonomy. The West Pakistani rulers responded by launching a vicious military crackdown. Bangladesh's bloody birth trauma began. As the Bengalis waged a guerilla struggle and millions of refugees poured across the border into India, Bangladesh was suddenly catapulted from relative obscurity into the headlines of the world press. The Indian government, straining under the refugee burden and worried lest the liberation struggle assume more radical overtones, finally sent its army into Bangladesh in December, and the Pakistanis surrendered two weeks later.

Independence brought hope that the country, freed at last from the shackles of colonial domination, could begin to develop its abundant resources and address the needs of its people. But beneath the euphoria of independence lurked the deeply rooted problems of economic stagnation and impoverishment. When we arrived in Dacca in 1974, the triumphant flush of enthusiasm had faded, giving way to growing anger and despair. Many Bengalis blamed soaring rice prices and the autumn famine on the corruption of Mujib's ruling party, and on the hoarding of grain by merchants. A Dacca rickshaw puller told us, "First the English robbed us. Then the Pakistanis robbed us. Now we are being robbed by our own people."

Since independence Bangladesh has received a massive influx of foreign aid—over $1 billion per year. Yet the country's agriculture and industry continue to stagnate and the living conditions of the poor steadily deteriorate. Bangladesh's colonial legacy cannot be easily erased. The British and Pakistani rulers may be gone, but they left a social order which condemns millions to needless hunger.

Villager carries paddy seedlings to the field for transplanting. *Photo by Hartman/Boyce.*

3. Who Owns the Land?

The pattern of landownership in Bangladesh profoundly affects both the production and distribution of food. Although Bangladesh is often called a "land of small farmers," the reality in the villages is more complex. On the one hand, many villagers own no land at all and depend upon wage labor for their livelihoods. On the other hand are landlords whose holdings, though modest by American standards, are large enough to free them from the necessity of working in the fields.

A recent study commissioned by the United States Agency for International Development (AID) found that a "dichotomy between ownership of land and labor on it" is widespread in Bangladesh. Less than 10 percent of Bangladesh's rural households own over half the country's cultivable land, while 60 percent of rural families own less than 10 percent of the land. One third own no cultivable land at all, and by including those who own less than half an acre, the study concludes that 48 percent of the families of rural Bangladesh are "functionally landless." Pointing to the difficulties of collecting reliable data, the authors of the study note that these figures probably *underestimate* the actual extent of landlessness and the true level of concentration of landownership.[1]

Based on their different relationships to the land, the villagers of Bangladesh fall into five basic classes:

- **Landlords** do not work on the land themselves, except sometimes to supervise their workers. Instead they hire labor or let out land to sharecroppers.
- **Rich peasants** work in the fields but have more land than they can cultivate alone. They gain most of their income from lands they cultivate with hired labor or sharecroppers.
- **Middle peasants** come closest to our image of the self-sufficient small farmer. They earn their livings mainly by working their own land, though at times they may work for others or hire others to work for them.
- **Poor peasants** own a little land, but not enough to support themselves. They earn their livings mainly by working as sharecroppers or wage laborers.
- **Landless laborers** own no land except for their house sites, and sometimes not even that. Lacking draft animals and agricultural implements, they seldom can work as sharecroppers, and must depend upon wages for their livelihoods.

A villager in Katni told us, "Without land, there is no security." Indeed, without land there is often no food. An International Labor Organization study reports that landless laborers consume only 78 percent as much grain as those who own over seven and one-half acres of land, despite the fact that the landless need 40 percent more calories because they work harder.[2] As we shall see, landownership not only determines who will have enough to eat, but also affects how much food is actually produced.

Not surprisingly, the small minority of rural families who own over half the country's farmland are, in the words of the AID study, "at the apex of the structure of power in rural Bangladesh; the

"Land, the ultimate source of wealth and power in rural Bangladesh, is becoming concentrated in fewer and fewer hands."

political economy of the countryside is controlled by them."[3] Land is the key to their power, power which in turn brings them control over other food-producing resources such as irrigation facilities and fertilizer. Since these agricultural inputs are often highly subsidized by the government, they are all the more desirable to the rural elite.

Similarly, the large landowner is better able to receive low interest loans from government banks. His land serves as collateral, and he knows how to deal with the bank officials: how to fill out the necessary forms and when to propose a snack at the nearest tea stall. The large landowners also usually dominate village cooperatives which have access to government credit.

The rural poor meanwhile must turn to the village moneylender when they need cash, often paying interest rates of more than 100 percent a year. Not coincidentally, the moneylender and the large landowner are often one and the same person. Since Islam, Bangladesh's main religion, condemns the taking of interest, moneylenders ease their consciences through such simple expedients as buying a peasant's crop before the harvest—at half the market rate. To get credit small farmers frequently mortgage their land, forfeiting the right to cultivate it until they repay the loan.

The large landowners' control of food-producing resources—land, inputs and credit—allows them to appropriate much of the wealth produced in the countryside. As a result, they are able to buy out hard-pressed smaller farmers, driving them into the ever growing ranks of the landless. One study found that peasants who own less than an acre of land sell half their remaining land every year.[4] Land, the ultimate source of wealth and power in rural Bangladesh, is becoming concentrated in fewer and fewer hands.

Shaha Paikur: Landlord, Merchant and Moneylender

Shaha Paikur lives with his four wives in a cement house in Dosutari, a village adjoining Katni. He is typical of the local merchants, for he is also a landlord and moneylender. He deals in jute, rice and mustard seed, and his warehouse is large enough to hold the produce of many local peasants as well as that of his own extensive landholdings. When he sells his jute, a caravan of 50 oxcarts carries it to town. Villagers often speculate about his riches, and some claim he buries gold in his courtyard.

Shaha Paikur's moneylending has earned him an unsavory reputation. "He began life with nothing but a sharp eye," recalls our neighbor Aktar Ali. "First he married an orphan girl who had some land, and then he worked himself up by moneylending, charging interest rates so high that borrowers could seldom pay him back. When we first came here, he took some of our land too. Now we have learned never to borrow from him; when in need, we borrow from our relatives.

"Shaha is clever, though. When a man falls on hard times, Shaha offers money. He acts so friendly, 'You have no rice? You have no clothes? Here, take this! You can pay me back at harvest time.'

"Men are weak. They know they shouldn't take his money, but they think: 'Let me eat today. Let the future bring what it may.' At harvest time Shaha is back, demanding payment in rice at half the market rate. When a man cannot repay, Shaha takes his land—he never lends money to a landless man.

"Our *Koran* tells us that moneylending is a great sin. In Allah's eyes, taking interest is as evil as murder. Let me tell you a story to prove it. Last year, when caterpillars attacked my rice crop, I tried all kinds of chemical sprays with no effect. Finally someone suggested the old method of writing a moneylender's name on pieces of paper and tying them to stakes at three corners of the field. You leave one corner open so the insects can escape. I wrote Shaha Paikur's name, tied it to the stakes, and in two days those caterpillars were gone! That is how much Allah despises the moneylender—even pests flee his name!"

Today the villagers are wary of Shaha Paikur's advances, and turn to him for money only in desperation. But Shaha has found other avenues to expand his fortune. He is now the biggest landlord in Dosutari, with holdings scattered in neighboring villages. At harvest time his agents ply the local markets and his warehouse fills. When the price is right an oxcart caravan takes his goods to town. He sells jute to the government and to bigger merchants, rice to the grain dealers in the nearest town, and mustard seed to a company which presses it for oil. With his profits he buys more land.

Although trade is not as morally repugnant as moneylending, many villagers resent Shaha Paikur as much for his merchant activities as for his usury. "I grow the jute in Shaha's warehouse," said one middle peasant. "Without me, where would he be? What do I get for my labor? Worn hands, aching muscles, and just enough to eat so that I can live to work another day. Meanwhile Shaha sits and eats, and counts his *taka*."

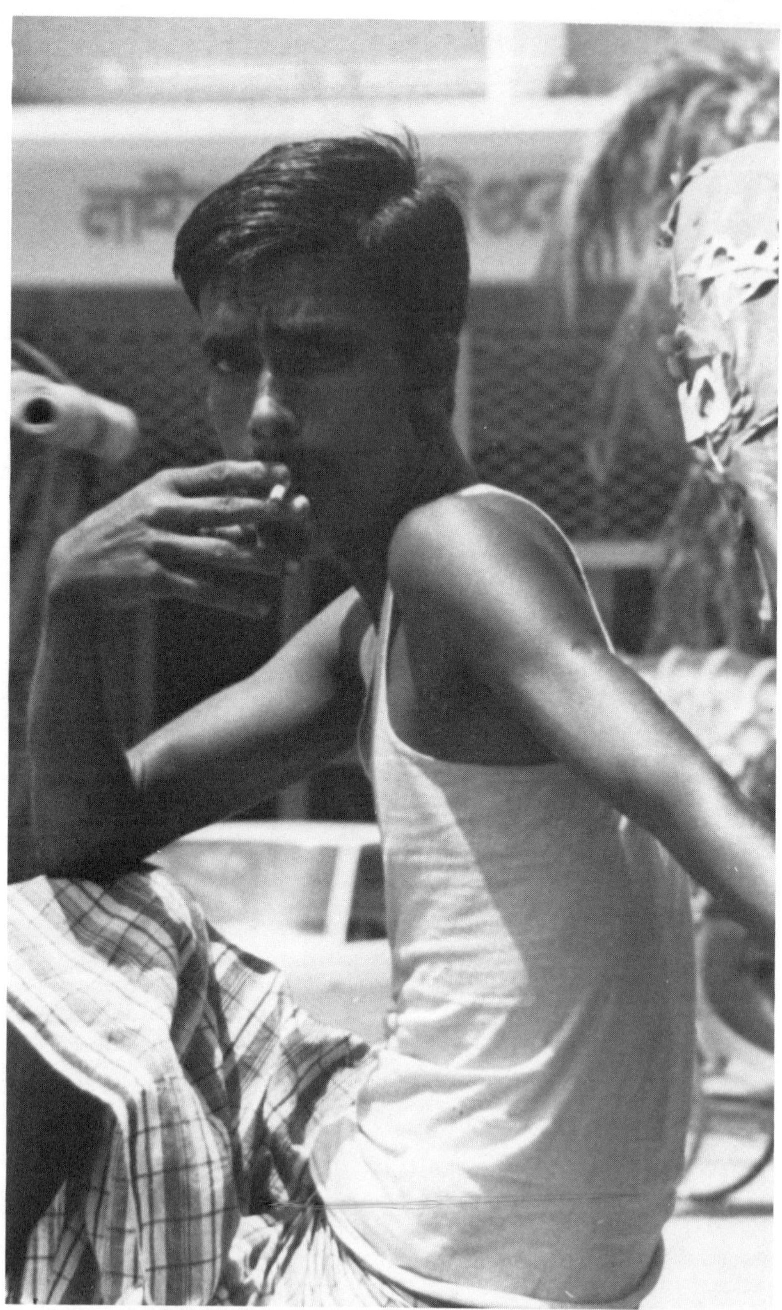

Cycle rickshaw puller in Dacca. *Photo by Benedict Tisa.*

4. Siphoning the Surplus

Just as Bangladesh is often called a land of small farmers, so the country's agriculture is sometimes described as "subsistence farming." The implication is that the peasants grow barely enough to feed themselves, with little left over for anyone else. Once again, reality is more complex. Much of the wealth which the peasants produce in the fields is siphoned by large landowners, moneylenders and merchants. The hunger of Bangladesh's poor majority is intimately related to the ways this wealth is extracted and used.

Who Works, Who Eats?

Surplus is siphoned from poor peasants and landless laborers by the twin mechanisms of sharecropping and wage labor, production relationships which determine who works the land and who eats its fruits.

Sharecropping, according to a 1977 AID study, covers at least 23 percent of Bangladesh's farmland.[1] In Katni's vicinity, landlords and rich peasants generally cultivate about three-fourths of their land by means of sharecroppers and the remaining one-fourth with hired labor. The landowner and sharecropper normally split the crop equally, although in some districts the landowner often takes two-thirds.[2] The sharecropper usually must bear the costs of seed and fertilizer, so that in practice his share is really less than half the crop.

Although the rewards from sharecropping may seem meager, those of wage labor are even less. In Katni the standard wage for male laborers is about 33 U.S. cents per day, paid in a combination of rice, cash and a morning meal which insures that the laborer has enough strength to work all day in the fields. Women from poor families who work processing crops in well-to-do households earn even less—about 20 cents for a day's hard labor.

The number of landless laborers in Bangladesh is rising rapidly due to population growth and the displacement of small farmers. The dramatic rise in landlessness has not been matched by a rise in employment opportunities. As a result, in 1974 real wages for agricultural laborers had fallen to less than two-thirds of their 1963 level.[3] As Dalim, a landless laborer, told us: "I earn two pounds of rice, one *taka* (about 7 cents) and a meal for a day's work. With that *taka* I used to be able to buy two more pounds of rice, with a little left over for oil, chilis and salt. But today one *taka* won't even buy one pound of rice. Employers used to let their workers take a few free vegetables when they went home in the evening, but nowadays they aren't so generous. Times are getting harder for men like me."

With wages declining, it is becoming more profitable for the landowner to cultivate with hired labor than to give land to sharecroppers. The large landowners in Katni's vicinity calculate that wage labor only costs them one-fourth to one-third of the crop. They are slowly shifting more and more land to hired labor.

In some countries this shift has been associated with the "green revolution"—the introduction of new crop varieties, chemical fertilizers and irrigation—which by raising yields also makes wage labor more attractive to the landowner than sharecropping. But in Katni the main reason for the shift is not that yields are going up, but rather that wages are going down.

Poor peasants and landless laborers are caught on an economic treadmill. No matter how hard they run they keep slipping backwards. The siphoning of the surplus makes it almost impossible for them to save enough money to buy land of their own. Instead, illness and unemployment often force them to sell their remaining tiny plots of land and their meager household possessions (*The Trials of A Poor Peasant Family,* p. 27). Though they devote their lives to growing and processing food, they face perpetual hunger.

What happens to the surplus once it passes into the landowners' hands? If it were used productively, the suffering of the poor might not be entirely in vain. After all, any society must generate a surplus for investment if the economy is to grow. But in Bangladesh very little of the surplus finds its way into productive investment. Luxury consumption absorbs much of the income of the rural elite. For example, Nafis, a big landlord, bought himself a new Japanese motorcycle while we were in Katni. It cost him as much as a laborer working on his land would earn in 20 years.

Large landowners are reluctant to invest in agriculture, for farming is a difficult and risky business. They may buy more land, but this is simply a transfer of resources (usually from small farmers), which adds nothing to the nation's productive base. Even less of the surplus is mobilized for investment elsewhere in the economy through taxes or savings because the government does not want to tax the large landowners for fear of losing their political support, and the interest paid on savings deposits cannot compare with other more profitable uses to which the landowner can put his money. Trade and moneylending—both of which siphon surplus from the peasants while leaving the production process untouched—offer by far the most lucrative and easy avenues for investment.

The Market

Through the exchanges of the marketplace, merchants are able to siphon surplus from Bangladesh's peasants. Receiving low prices for the crops they sell and often paying high prices for the goods they buy, the peasants lose whether they enter the market as producers or as consumers. The transfer of wealth is often hidden by the seemingly impersonal movement of prices, but in Katni we found several examples which throw the relationship between peasants and merchants into sharp relief.

Photo by Hartmann/Boyce.

"In Bangladesh we call our jute 'the golden fiber,' " said one peasant. "But tell me, who gets the gold?"

Jute, the fiber used to make rope, burlap and carpet backing, is the main cash crop of Bangladesh's peasants and provides about four-fifths of the country's export earnings. After independence jute prices stagnated, while rice prices soared. As a result, peasants grew less jute and more rice, so that by 1975 jute acreage had shrunk to two-thirds of its pre-independence level. Worried about export earnings, the government announced a floor price for jute which it hoped would check the decline in production. Government purchasing centers throughout the country were instructed to buy jute from the growers for about 90 *taka* per *maund* (one *maund* is about 80 pounds).

One such purchasing center was located three miles from Katni. Nevertheless, the villagers sold their jute in the local markets for 60 *taka* per *maund*, two-thirds of the government rate. At this price jute was decidedly a losing venture. As the rich peasant Kamal complained: "I sold my jute for less than half of what it cost me to grow it!"

A visit to the local jute procurement center yielded some clues as to the reasons for the striking discrepancy between the official support price and the actual market rate received by the peasants. The purchasing center consisted of a half dozen large warehouse buildings which had once belonged to a West Pakistani company. The buildings were piled high with rough bales and loose mounds of the golden fiber.

The manager, a heavyset young man dressed in Western clothing, was happy to explain how the jute is graded and how to operate the baling press. But when asked where the jute in his warehouse came from, his reply was guarded: "We buy from the growers."

"At what price?"

"We pay the government rate, 91.50 *taka* per *maund.*"

"How curious. In the markets a few miles from here, the growers are selling their jute for only 60 *taka.*"

"Oh, they must be selling to the merchants."

"Ah, the merchants. And do you buy from them too?"

"Yes, we buy from the licensed traders." The manager stressed the word "licensed," to emphasize the legitimacy of such transactions.

"The jute in this warehouse—did you buy most of it from growers, or from merchants?"

The manager began to look uneasy. "Well, actually we buy mostly from the merchants. You see, these growers only bring in eight or ten *maunds* at a time, so it is very inconvenient to buy from them. From the merchants we can buy hundreds of *maunds* at once."

The manager declined to elaborate as to why the growers are willing to sell so cheaply in the local markets, if they could receive the much higher government price simply by coming to the warehouse a few miles away. The villagers were less reticent. "If I bring in a cartload of jute," said one middle peasant, "the warehouse people say, 'Today we are closed—come back tomorrow.' So my time has been wasted. If I return the next day they will have another excuse: 'We've already bought our quota for the day,' or 'We have to wait for funds from Dacca.' We can never sell our jute to the government."

Why do the warehouse people turn the peasants away? Our middle peasant friend explained: "We sell our jute in the market at 60 *taka.* The merchants then sell it to the government at 90 *taka,* making a 30 *taka* profit on each *maund.* They share this profit with the warehouse manager, giving him maybe half. So of course he won't buy from us!" Besides paying kickbacks, the merchants are said to pay the warehouse manager a monthly retainer in order to ensure his cooperation. The manager accordingly buys only from those who make it "convenient" for him to do so. Perhaps he does buy directly from a few growers—local landlords who make suitable arrangements.

In previous years jute prices in the local markets had been somewhat higher, because much jute was smuggled to India and this demand had helped to keep prices up. But in 1975, following the assassination of Sheikh Mujib, the political connections which had protected the smugglers unraveled and the illegal flow of jute across the border slowed to a trickle. In collusion with the government authorities, a few merchants were then able to strengthen their control over the local jute market, pushing prices to the abysmally low level of 60 *taka* per *maund.*

"In Bangladesh we call our jute 'the golden fiber,' " said one peasant. "But tell me, who gets the gold?"

While some merchants buy cash crops from the peasants, others sell various goods to them. No villager is entirely self-sufficient; all rely on the market to meet some of their needs. Landless laborers and poor peasants must buy food, everyone has to buy salt and cloth, and those who can afford them purchase such items as medicine and footwear. The prices the villagers pay are often high, in part because of hoarding by merchants.

Sometimes hoarding is a reaction to genuine scarcities, but other times it is a means to deliberately raise prices. Merchants not only manage at times to control the supply of a particular good within a given locality; on occasion they are able to corner a market throughout the country. For example, in the autumn of 1974 a cartel cornered the market for salt in Bangladesh. The price rose to 50 times its normal level, and salt riots broke out in major towns. For two weeks the merchants who hoarded the nation's salt reaped tremendous profits. Then they loosened their grip, and prices returned to normal.

Most hoarding is less spectacular, and it is often hard to say where natural scarcities end and artificial ones begin. For example, rice prices are generally lowest at harvest time and highest just before the next harvest. This predictable fluctuation makes speculation in rice attractive to merchants. If they hold stocks in anticipation of rising prices, this in itself helps to lift prices. Landless laborers and poor peasants, who rely on the market for much of their food needs, must pay the price. Middle peasants often lose coming and going: they sell their rice cheaply at harvest time because they need cash for consumption, investment in the next crop and repayment of debts; a few months later they have to buy rice at inflated prices.

The rice trade was not particularly lucrative in the 1960s, but after independence this changed. In 1974 the price of rice climbed to 10 times its pre-independence level. Peasants were particularly vulnerable in parts of the country where floods had damaged crops. As prices rose, many sold their animals, their land and their household possessions in order to buy rice. The poorest, with nothing left to sell, came to the towns in search of work or relief. An estimated 100,000 people starved to death.

A villager recalls: "Lalganj (a town five miles from Katni) became a town of beggars. Whole families were living, sleeping and dying in the streets. Each day there were new bodies along the roadside."

Officially, the government blamed the famine on floods, but many observers believed that hoarding by merchants and a breakdown in government administration were responsible for turning a manageable, localized shortage into a catastrophe. According to an AID official in Dacca: "The food supply was there; it just didn't get to the right people."

The 1974 famine brought terrible suffering to many people, but to some it brought profit. The merchants who hoarded grain were not the only ones to benefit. Moneylenders did a brisk business, and large landowners were able to buy land cheaply from their poor neighbors. In the hardest hit areas land registry offices had to stay open late into the night to handle the record sales.

The villagers are well acquainted with many of the merchants who profit at their expense. The men who buy their jute, for example, are local landlords who have diversified into trade and moneylending (*Shaha Paikur: Landlord, Merchant and Moneylender*, p. 19). A pyramid of trade extends above these local merchants to regional, national and sometimes even international economic interests. At the base of this pyramid are the peasants. They sum up their situation with a simple phrase: "The merchants drink our blood."

The Trials of A Poor Peasant Family

Hartmann/Boyce

Abu and Sharifa live with their six children in a one-room bamboo house with broken walls and a leaky straw roof. They are poor peasants, and year by year they are becoming poorer.

"I wasn't born this way," says Abu. "When I was a boy I never went hungry. My father had to sell some land during the '43 famine, but still we had enough. We moved to Katni when he died—my mother, myself, and my three brothers. We bought an acre and a half of land. As long as none of us brothers married that was enough, but one by one we married and divided the land."

"I was young," recalls Sharifa, "and I worked very hard. I husked rice in other women's houses to earn money, and finally I saved enough for us to buy another half acre of land. But my husband's mother was old and dying, and he wanted to spend my money to buy medicines for her. He threatened to divorce me if I didn't give him the money, so I gave in. The money was wasted—she died anyway—and we were left with less than half an acre. Then the children came. Our situation grew worse and worse, and we often had to borrow to eat. Sometimes our neighbors lent us a few *taka,* but many times we had to sell our rice to moneylenders before the harvest. They paid us in advance and then took the rice at half its value."

"People get rich in this country by taking interest," Abu interjects bitterly. "They have no fear of Allah—they care only for this life. When they buy our rice they say they aren't taking interest but really they are."

"No matter how hard we worked," continues Sharifa, "we never had enough money. We started selling things—our wooden bed, our cattle, our plow, our wedding gifts. Finally we began to sell the land."

Today Abu and Sharifa own less than one-fifth of an acre of land. Most of this is mortgaged to Mahmud Hazi, a local landlord. Until Abu repays his debt, he must work his own land as a sharecropper, giving Mahmud Hazi half the crop. "I can't even earn enough to feed my family," he says, "let alone enough to pay off the mortgage."

Sharecropping is difficult. "When I work for wages," he explains, "at least we have rice, even if it's not enough to fill our stomachs. But I don't eat from my sharecropping until the harvest. To plow the land I have to rent oxen from a neighbor, plowing his land for two days in exchange for one day's use of his animals. In this country a man's labor is worth half as much as the labor of a pair of cows!"

When Sharifa can find work husking rice, she usually receives only a pound of rice for a day's labor. Often she cannot find employment. "If we had land I would always be busy," she says. "Husking rice, grinding lentils, cooking three times a day. Instead I have nothing to do, so I just watch the children and worry. What kind of life is that?" She unwraps a piece of betel nut from the corner of her *sari*. "Without this we poor people would never survive. Whenever I feel hungry I chew betel nut and it helps the pain in my stomach. I can go for days without food. It's only worrying about the children that makes me thin."

Soon after our arrival in Katni, Abu fell ill with a raging fever. For a month he was unable to work. Sharifa husked rice in other households and their children collected wild greens, but finally hunger and the need to buy medicine forced the family to sell another bit of land: three-hundredths of an acre. They slipped a little further towards total landlessness.

Six months later, in the lean season before the autumn harvest, Abu and Sharifa could not find any work. Again the family faced a crisis. "Sharifa will tell you she lost her gold nose pin," a neighbor whispered to Betsy. "It's a lie. If she had really lost it, her husband would be beating her. He sold it in the bazaar. How else would they be eating rice tonight?"

The money from the nose pin was soon gone, so one sunny afternoon Abu cut down the jackfruit tree beside his house. He had planted it four years earlier, and in another year it might have borne its first fruit. By selling it as firewood in town he hoped to get 25 *taka*. Sharifa and a young son watched as he dug up the roots, which he could also sell as fuel. "Do you know what it is like when your children are hungry?" asked Sharifa. "They cry because you can't feed them. I tell you, it's not easy to be a mother."

She brushed a strand of hair from her forehead and unconsciously fingered the small twig stuck in the hole where her nose pin used to be. "Why do you sit here listening to our troubles? When people in this country are happy and their bellies are full, they won't listen to tales of sorrow. They say, 'Why are you telling me this? I don't want to hear.' "

Abu nodded. "Our religion says that the rich man should care for the poor man. He should ask him whether he has eaten. But in this country a rich man won't even look at a poor man."

Sharifa gazed into the fields and mused aloud: "They say that Allah makes men rich and poor. But sometimes I wonder—is it Allah's work, or is it the work of men?"

Preparing a field for Bangladesh's main crop: transplanted rice. *Hartmann/Boyce.*

5. The Inefficiency of Inequality

From the pages of economic texts and the documents of government planners the familiar theme often emanates that inequalities in income distribution are economically efficient. We are led to believe that the concentration of wealth in the hands of a few leads to higher savings and investment, which ultimately benefits society as a whole. But a look at the realities of rural Bangladesh has already revealed that the surplus the elite extracts from the peasants is not invested productively. The squandering of wealth which could potentially finance development is only one side of the inefficiency of inequality in Bangladesh. The other side is the chronic underutilization of existing resources: land, labor and water.

Bigger isn't Better

In Bangladesh the concentration of land in the hands of a few large farmers is a major cause of low agricultural productivity. Several studies indicate that in Bangladesh, as in many countries, small farms have per acre yields equal to or higher than those of large farms. As one report noted: "This may be considered remarkable in view of the heavy discrimination against marginal farmers as far as distribution of modern inputs is concerned."[1] Even though they reap the advantages of subsidized fertilizer, irrigation and credit, Bangladesh's large farmers still don't produce more than their smaller neighbors!

The reasons for this discrepancy are not hard to fathom. The large landowners tend to cultivate their lands less intensively than small owners. The small landowning peasant, who tills the soil with his own hands, knows that his work determines how much he and his family will have to eat. He invests more labor in his agriculture, and strives to use every bit of land and every drop of water to its utmost. The large landowner's incentive is not so great, and the incentive of the sharecroppers and wage laborers who actually work his land is often minimal.

The sharecropper knows that half the fruits of his labor will go to the landowner, so he saves his extra effort for the little land he owns himself. He has little incentive to invest in agricultural inputs, not only because the landowner will reap half the benefits, but also because he knows that next year he may not be around to enjoy the returns to his investment. According to the AID land survey, more than 70 percent of all sharecroppers have cultivated their tenant lands for a period of three years or less. This leads the authors to conclude, "It may be reasonably assumed that with such a high turnover in tenant-operated areas that tenants might be less than enthusiastic concerning the need to invest in improvements in such land—including the use of fertilizers having residual impact in succeeding years."[2] The landowner also displays a marked reluctance to invest in improvements, for he has easier ways to make money. The AID study found that less than one percent of landowners supplied any inputs to their tenants.[3]

If the large landowner cultivates with hired labor, he may be more likely to invest in inputs, but once again yields are likely to be lower than if the same land were owned and tilled by a smaller farmer. Hired laborers have even less incentive to produce than sharecroppers: they worry about their wage, not about the landowner's yields. And since the landowner must pay for their labor, he uses it sparingly. Moreover, large landowners are often poor farm managers. They usually disdain the dirty work of farming, preferring instead to devote their entrepreneurial talents to such refined activities as trade and moneylending. The villagers of Katni described the incompetence of one big landlord: "Nafis understands nothing about farming. He seldom even goes to the fields. His workers cheat him all the time, and laugh at him behind his back."

Since small farmers cultivate their land more intensively, they also tend to make more efficient use of credit and agricultural inputs—when they can get them. But most of these resources flow to the large landowners, by virtue of their political power. Commenting on the Bangladesh government's latest rural credit scheme, the World Bank notes: "As usual for such programs, the small farmers demonstrated a better repayment record but did not get a large share of the credit outlays."[4]

While in Katni, we had the chance to see the government's agricultural extension service in action. One day the village children ran to tell us that a "foreigner" had come to see us. It turned out to be the local agricultural extension agent. With his immaculate clothing and upper-class accent, the children were sure he was not a Bengali. The agent's job was to give technical advice to farmers, but he was a stranger to the poor and middle peasants of Katni. We learned that his main role was simply apportioning subsidized fertilizer among the local landlords. These realities are what the AID study calls "institutional impediments" to the dissemination of new agricultural technology.

In Japan and Taiwan, the groundwork for a highly productive agriculture was a far-reaching land reform, which put control of food-producing resources into the hands of small farmers. In the absence of such a land reform, to imagine that one could redirect credit, inputs and agricultural extension services to the small farmers of Bangladesh is wishful thinking. Moreover, even if by some stroke of political magic one could reorient development programs in favor of the poor and middle peasants, this would still leave out the large and growing numbers of landless.

Underemployment of Labor

The chronic underemployment of Bangladesh's landless and poor peasants represents a terrible waste of the country's greatest resource: the labor of its people. The demand for agricultural labor is highly seasonal—in the peak periods of harvesting, weeding the spring rice and transplanting the rainy season rice, most of the poor can find work. But between these periods they are often unemployed, with no income at all. Taking these seasonal fluctuations into account, a United Nations study set the unemployment rate in rural Bangladesh at a staggering 42 percent.[5] For many, this figure translates into chronic hunger and even starvation (*The Death of A Landless Laborer,* p. 36).

Massive underemployment means that millions of people cannot afford to buy basic consumer goods. This lack of what economists call "effective demand" is in itself a cause of economic stagnation. Industry cannot grow without a market, but families who can hardly afford to eat are not about to become consumers of even basic items such as footwear and soap. Indeed, their lack of buying power may act as a brake on food production too. Discussing the prospect of rising unemployment, a cable from AID's Dacca mission states, "These findings in turn cast doubt upon the feasibility of current foodgrain production strategies, implying as they do a general reduction in the level of demand."[6]

The rural poor of Bangladesh represent a huge, untapped work force for labor-intensive agricultural and industrial projects. Mobilized for development, they could be transformed from a drain on the nation's economy into a powerful asset. Yet despite the fact that labor-intensive rural works projects are frequently endorsed as a key to development in Bangladesh, efforts to implement such projects run aground on hard political realities; the government has other priorities. As the AID cable notes: "The government's Rural Works Program is widely reported to have been in a state of deterioration in recent years owing to a variety of management difficulties."[7]

For their part, the rural poor have no incentive to undertake such projects as long as they are deprived of the land which would be improved by their labor. Even if more rural works projects were instituted, the extent to which the landless would benefit is open to question. As an AID study points out:

> Such projects (e.g., the building of a farm to market road) provide income to rural workers for a specified period, but do nothing generally to change the fundamental economic conditions that produced unemployment in the first place. At the same time, such projects tend to provide long-term benefits to landholders who, in this example, use the road to gain access to local markets.[8]

In the same vein, the World Bank warns that the scope for reducing unemployment and poverty through rural works projects "would be offset by the inequitable distribution of secondary benefits of the program."[9] As one experienced Bank official told us, "It's hard to see much we can really do for the landless." Hard, that is, under the present inequitable social order.

Water, Water Everywhere, But . . .

The present structure of landownership in Bangladesh results in the underutilization of another precious agricultural resource: water. Although Bangladesh has vast surface and ground water resources, only 12 percent of the country's cropland is currently irrigated. Irrigation would bring tremendous production increases in the dry winter season, would insure the regular spring and monsoon season crops against drought, and would allow earlier plantings which reduce the risk of flood damage. But today the uneven distribution and fragmentation of landholdings blocks the cooperative effort needed to harness Bangladesh's great water resources.

Although it would be a formidable engineering challenge, there is certainly great potential for taming Bangladesh's rivers through construction of dams, embankments and canals. These could provide not only irrigation but also much-needed flood control and drainage for millions of acres. Bangladesh has no shortage of manpower to undertake these tasks but, as we have seen, the mobilization of this labor is almost impossible under the present social order. Moreover, the fact that land is fragmented into many

---

"The chronic underemployment of Bangladesh's landless and poor peasants represents a terrible waste of the country's greatest resource: the labor of its people."

---

individual holdings poses great difficulties for any such scheme. For instance, who would decide whose precious plots would be sacrificed to the construction of canals and channels?

Indeed, fragmentation and unequal distribution of landholdings today undermine even modest efforts to provide irrigation with low-lift pumps and tubewells. For example, a deep tubewell can irrigate 60 acres of land. But even the biggest landlords seldom own so much in a single block—their holdings are scattered here and there. So to use such a well to its full capacity requires cooperation, which is hard to come by as long as a few large landowners control irrigation resources for their own benefit. An AID cable points to "the well known fact that pump group cooperatives exist only on paper or are otherwise captured by the large landowners."[10]

The World Bank, which has financed several tubewell projects in Bangladesh, has found persistent "organizational problems arising in conveying the water to the farmers' fields."[11] They are pouring an extra million dollars into one deep tubewell project to facilitate the digging of water channels. "You or I could go out there and dig those channels," one Bank official admitted. "The problem is not that the farmers don't know how to dig ditches, but that they don't want to." In rural Bangladesh political realities not only make large-scale irrigation works impossible—even the use of a single tubewell is problematic!

The Priorities of the Elite

There is another important dimension to the inefficiency of inequality in Bangladesh. The priorities of the government reflect the interests of a narrow elite rather than the needs of the poor majority. For instance, expenditures for "defense, justice and police" have risen from 20 percent of the revenue budget under Sheikh Mujib to 30 percent under the present regime of Major-General Ziaur Rahman.[12] Government leaders meanwhile make innumerable pronouncements about the importance of attaining agricultural self-sufficiency. But although agriculture generates almost 60 percent of the Gross National Product (GNP) and employs over 80 percent of the labor force, its share of the government's development budget is scheduled to drop from 30 percent in 1976-78 to 25 percent in 1979-80.[13] And the little money devoted to agriculture will mainly be used to subsidize the price of fertilizer.

Agriculture suffers not only from a lack of funds, but from a lack of commitment on the part of government officials. The World Bank notes pointedly: "Examples of the few countries which have been successful in rural development (e.g. China, Taiwan and Korea) show that government officials have diligently and persistently worked with local people."[14] In Bangladesh, even the most optimistic foreign aid officials admit this diligence and persistence in rural development is hard to come by. The concept of public service is alien to most members of Bangladesh's elite, who look upon the poor majority with disdain. For them, villages are to be escaped, not to be served.

In fact, the main development which has taken place in Bangladesh in recent years is the development of the elite. Bangladesh's most pressing employment problem is providing work for the millions of landless rural people, but as the World Bank reports, "The only sector which has been booming in terms of employment is public administration."[15] While real wages of landless laborers are plummeting, the government recently increased the salaries of civil servants by 20 to 25 percent.[16]

Although Bangladesh suffers from a shortage of skilled workers, ranging from doctors to mechanics, the government is now encouraging such workers to go abroad so they will send home foreign exchange. (One reason the government needs foreign exchange is to repay foreign aid loans.) At present more than 3000 Bangladeshis migrate to the Middle East each month.[17] More of Bangladesh's senior nurses now work there than in their own country! The *New York Times* reports from Dacca that the mass exodus of skilled labor is "so serious that the Agency for International Development has all but stopped sending Bangladeshis to the United States for training, even though specialized skills are badly needed here to promote development."[18] Exporting labor which is needed at home is like exporting food when people are hungry: resources go where the profits are highest, not where the needs are greatest.

Hunger in Bangladesh is neither natural nor inevitable. Its causes are deeply rooted, but they are man-made. The surplus siphoned from the peasants is squandered; land, labor and water are underutilized; and, at the national level, financial resources and skilled manpower are allocated for the benefit of a few rather than for the well-being of the majority. Although we have painted a bleak picture, Bangladesh's future is by no means hopeless. Identifying the barriers to development is an important first step to formulating a positive alternative.

The Death of A Landless Laborer

Komla in front of her home. *Photo by Hartmann/Boyce.*

"Between the mortar and the pestle, the chili cannot last. We poor are like chilis. Each year we are ground down a little more, until there is nothing left of us."

These are the words of Hari, a Hindu landless laborer who lived in Katni with his wife Komla, their three young children, and a niece whose parents died in the 1974 famine. Their house consisted of a packed mud floor, a sagging straw roof and walls made of a few dried palm leaves hanging from bamboo poles. Inside there was no furniture—the family slept on burlap bags, covering themselves with straw on cold winter nights. Hari did not even own the land on which the house was built.

Hari's father once owned six acres, enough land to support his wife and five sons. He sold some land to pay for his sons' weddings, but most of it was stolen by powerful Muslim landowners who rose to fill the vacuum left by the departure of the Hindu *zamindar.* Through fraud, force and moneylending, men like Shaha Paikur wrested Hari's father's land.

At the time of his death, Hari's father owned only one acre of land, which was then divided among the five brothers. Hari's one-fifth of an acre was not enough to feed his growing family, so he worked as a wage laborer and Komla husked rice in other households. Little by little, Hari sold his land to buy food, clothing and medicine and to repay his debts. By 1971 the land was gone, but Hari and Komla still had a few objects of value—a wooden bed, and a house with solid walls of woven bamboo mats. Then came the independence war.

The Hindus of Katni had to flee to India to escape the ravages of the Pakistani army, for whom any Hindu was fair game. In the crowded refugee camps across the border, two of Hari's brothers died, probably of cholera. In retrospect, Hari said he had more to eat in the camps than he did when he returned to Bangladesh. Still he told us, "If we Hindus ever have to flee again, I'll just stay here. Everyone has to die once, and I would rather do it at home."

When Hari and Komla returned to Katni after the war, they had nothing. Their house had been looted; even the walls had been stolen. Despite the promises of government officials, they received no relief—

no food, no clothing, no blankets. Echoing poor people throughout Bangladesh, they maintained that corrupt local leaders sold these relief goods on the black market. Hari and Komla struggled to make ends meet, but rising rice prices cut into the value of their already meager wages.

In the autumn of 1974, when rice sold at 10 times its pre-independence level, Hari and Komla came face-to-face with famine. "I had no work, and we had nothing to eat," Hari recalled. "We begged from house to house, but no one had much to give. One day when I went to town, I saw hundreds of poor people living in the streets. The gutters were filled with their excrement. What an awful stench! People sat outside restaurants waiting for the cook to throw out a few scraps. I saw people fighting over the intestines of a chicken. I saw people selling their children in the bazaar."

"Later the government set up a gruel kitchen in the town. One day I went with my brother Kirot. We waited all day, and each got one *roti* (a piece of unleavened bread). Who can live on one *roti* a day? I decided I would rather die here than in town. My wife and I collected wild greens and roots, and when we weren't looking for food, we slept. When the children's cries woke us, we went out again to search for food. Kirot and his wife died at the gruel kitchen. That's why their daughter Gopi lives with us now."

The famine had passed by the time we arrived in Katni, but Hari and Komla were still living dangerously close to the margin. During the planting and harvesting of the crops they could find work, but in the slack seasons they often went for days without a decent meal. Hari's health slowly deteriorated. He was trapped in a vicious cycle: without work he could not eat, not eating made him weak, and because he was weak, employers did not want to hire him.

In the lean season before the autumn harvest of 1975, rice prices were unusually low because hoarders had unloaded their rice stocks in the uncertainty following Sheikh Mujib's assassination. But the low prices did not help Hari, who had no cash. Komla spent hours foraging for edible weeds and roots, while Hari searched from village to village for work. They sent their children to the town bazaar to collect the grains which spilled around the rice merchants' stalls. As the cool, damp nights of winter set in, Hari caught a cold. His body, weakened by hunger, could not resist it. Within a week he was dead.

Komla's face was knit in a permanent expression of despair. Villagers promised her work after the harvest, and some gave her a little rice when she begged at their houses, but their generosity was limited by their own poverty. Komla worried about her *sari*, which was falling to pieces. "This *sari* will last another month, no longer," she told Betsy. "What will I wear after that? How will I leave my house to look for work? My husband never earned much, but at least he shared my worries. Now I have to face the world alone."

Komla realized she would share the same fate as the other beggar women who passed through Katni—a life of unrelenting hunger. "People say I will die like my husband, like his brothers and their wives," she confided. "But until then I must try to feed the children."

Siddique carries a jackfruit to a local market. *Photo by Hartmann/Boyce.*

6. What is the Alternative?

With fertile land, abundant water and and vast reserves of natural gas, Bangladesh clearly has the potential to afford all its citizens a decent livelihood. The basic obstacles to realizing this potential are social, not technical. True, agricultural output can be increased somewhat by providing more inputs, more credit and better extension services, and by raising prices to give large landowners more incentive to produce. But this will not help those who have no land on which to grow food and are too poor to buy it; in fact, such production increases may actually result in greater hunger by accelerating the concentration of land in fewer hands. Moreover, the inefficiencies inherent in an inequitable social structure will continue to seriously limit the scope for increasing production.

Social Reconstruction

What is the alternative to the needless hunger of Bangladesh's poor majority? Only a far-reaching social reconstruction can break the fundamental barriers to increased production and at the same time ensure that the poor majority shares in the fruits of development. The key to such a reconstruction is land reform. If a ceiling of 10 acres per family were perfectly implemented and the excess land redistributed among the landless, each family would receive less than 0.4 acre. A more drastic four-acre ceiling would yield enough surplus to provide each landless and near landless family with a total of 0.86 acre.[1] But even if such a radical reform were implemented, over time lands would be subdivided among children, and for one reason or another some peasants would end up selling out to others, so that eventually a landless group would reemerge. This suggests that land reform, though necessary, would not alone be sufficient to overcome the roots of poverty in Bangladesh. Access to the land is only half of the answer to the needs of the rural poor; the other half lies in the cooperative use of the land.

Cooperation in agricultural production would enable the peasants of Bangladesh to undertake self-help development projects which remain impossible as long as agriculture is organized on a fragmented, individual basis. Through labor-intensive construction of irrigation facilities, drainage canals and embankments, the peasants could collectively begin to master the forces of nature in the face of which single individuals are powerless. As the people of our village remarked: "One bamboo alone is weak; many bamboos lashed together are unbreakable." The certainty that the peasants themselves would reap the fruits of their labor, rather than the village landlords, would release tremendous popular energy and initiative.

Western experts tend to disparage such an alternative approach to development. The authors of the AID land study, for example, dismiss this possibility:

> It is difficult to imagine the people in the countryside (even the landless), committed as they are by tradition to venerate individual rights in land, being amenable to joint farming activities of any kind. Only under circumstances in which the state was able and willing to employ extraordinary coercive power can such joint farming cooperatives be envisaged in Bangladesh. Therefore, for reasons that are practical rather than ideological, joint farming cooperatives do not appear to be a viable option within a general program for rural development.[2]

But are joint farming cooperatives in Bangladesh really such a far-fetched idea? Certainly no one should underestimate the difficulties involved in such a major social transformation, but one must distinguish between difficulties and insurmountable obstacles.

The assertion that the peasants of Bangladesh are committed by tradition to "venerate individual rights in land" is an overstatement. Land ownership in Bangladesh has been far from stable. After 1947, the breakup of the *zamindari* system resulted in the transfer of ownership of three-fourths of the country's land to new hands.[3] It was through such transfers that many of the landlords in Katni's vicinity acquired their extensive landholdings. The peasants recall this with bitterness; they hardly venerate the landlords' rights to the land.

While we were in the village, we witnessed the constant turnover of land, the buying and selling through which small farmers are being gradually dispossessed. Certainly, land is more than just another commodity to the peasants of Bangladesh, for land ownership can spell the difference between survival and starvation. But this is a question of economic security, not of quasi-religious attitudes.

Furthermore, the notion of cooperation was far from alien to the peasants of our village. Many small landowners worked together in informal mutual aid groups. Five or six peasants would join together during the plowing, transplanting or weeding of the fields or at harvest time, working one day on one man's land, the next day on another's and so on. Mostly this was done by middle and poor peasants, but sometimes landless friends would join the group, being paid by whomever owned the land that was worked on a particular day. The villagers explained, "When you work alone, time passes slowly. Working in a group, we talk and sing and the work gets done much faster."

A transition to joint farming in Bangladesh would necessarily pass through stages, perhaps building at first upon the existing tradition of mutual aid groups. It would have to rely on the peasants' own initiative—it could never be *imposed upon* them. Once convinced that change was possible, the landless and small farmers could be expected to actively support land redistribution and the growth of agricultural cooperation, for these would bring them improved living standards and greater control over their lives and labor.

Rich landowners would probably be less than enthusiastic about such changes, and force might be necessary to break their resistance. Coercion and the violence of state repression, as well as the more subtle violence of starvation, are today routine in Bangladesh. What would be "extraordinary" about any coercion involved in a social reconstruction would not be its scale but rather that it would be employed against the wealthy minority, instead of against the poor majority.

Who could exercise the necessary force to bring about a basic land reform? Only the poor themselves, whose numbers give them strength. The act of joining together to bring about social change would help to set the stage for cooperation in agricultural production itself. Industry as well as agriculture would benefit from such a social reconstruction, since those who today are too poor to buy consumer goods would be transformed into a vast internal market.

To suggest that the road to development in Bangladesh lies in this direction is not to say that the "Chinese model" can or should be exactly duplicated. The people of each country must chart their own path of development. What the Chinese have shown is that change is not impossible and that starvation is not inevitable. Development is a great challenge, and one which can only be met through the mobilization of the talents and energies of the poor

---

"Only far reaching social reconstruction can break the fundamental barriers to increased production and at the same time insure that the poor majority shares in the fruits of development. The key to such a reconstruction is land reform."

---

themselves. It will take patience, organization and dedication. There are no magic words and no instant solutions.

Too Optimistic?

Some might argue that this scenario is too optimistic. A World Bank staff member told us, "The poor people I knew would not be able to mobilize themselves for development or revolution. In Latin America maybe, but the poor in Bangladesh are too submissive and ignorant."

Privately, however, many aid officials view a far-reaching social reconstruction in Bangladesh not as a wishful dream but rather as a sad inevitability. AID's Dacca mission states in a 1978 memorandum: "More pessimistically, we foresee that the time will come when the organization of productive forces will have to be radically transformed in such a fashion that rural people will only be able to find security, employment and income in some form of communal agriculture."[4]

Are Bangladesh's peasants too "submissive and ignorant" to see the need for change? Bangladesh has a long history of peasant rebellions.[5] In 1947 and 1971 the peasants saw that political power can and does change hands. But to struggle against the rural elite is to invite retaliation. The large landowners are backed when necessary by the force of arms. Peasants are not by nature passive; on the contrary, they are among the most energetic, hardworking people in the world. The problem lies not in their ability to act, but in the powerful forces that prevent them from acting.

The rural elite which rules the countryside is not the only obstacle to change. The urban elite which controls the government also benefits from the present social order and wishes to preserve it. Moreover, in Bangladesh most members of the urban upper and middle classes are first or second generation city dwellers with roots still in the villages. The urban and rural elites are not only natural allies, they are also blood relations. Government patronage to the large landowners, in the form of subsidized inputs, credit and funds for local public works projects, serves to strengthen this alliance. The cross fertilization of the two elites has recently taken a new twist, as reported by *The Washington Post:* "Many of the land transfers recently recorded are to army officers, senior bureaucrats and police."[6]

There is no natural barrier to the satisfaction of the basic human needs of Bangladesh's people. But there is the man-made barrier of a social order which benefits a few at the expense of many. In the cautious language of an AID report, "A local government may lack the political will to implement needed agrarian reforms, however obvious the need for such reforms."[7] No such shortage of political will however is likely to handicap the government when it comes to crushing any challenge to the vested interests it protects.

Just as Bangladesh's large landowners rely on the backing of the elite-based government, so the government relies on financial and logistical support from wealthier countries. Each year the

United States government and U.S.-supported multilateral institutions provide hundreds of millions of dollars of foreign aid to the Bangladesh government. If we as Americans are concerned about the needless hunger of Bangladesh's poor majority, our first duty is to understand the effects of the aid given in our name.

US AND THEM

One of the World Bank's deep tubewells at work in northwest Bangladesh. According to the Bank, "production and employment opportunities are being increased" by the project. *World Bank photo by Tomas Sennett.*

7. Foreign Aid: A Helping Hand?

Foreign aid is big business in Bangladesh. The vehicles of aid agencies ply the streets of Dacca, their offices buzz with activity, and new luxury housing to accomodate their personnel sprouts in Dacca's suburbs. Although private voluntary agencies, of which there are more than one hundred in Bangladesh, are highly visible, they account for only four percent of the aid flowing into the country. The other 96 percent comes from official government agencies and international organizations.

Independence launched Bangladesh on its aid bonanza. Within three years of its break with Pakistan, the nation received $2.5 billion in aid commitments, more than it had received in its 25 years as East Pakistan. The flow is increasing: in fiscal year 1979 new aid commitments are projected to reach $1.6 billion.[1] Much of this aid comes from the United States and U.S.-supported multilateral institutions, such as the World Bank. Aid currently finances about half of the government's budget, and is equivalent to nearly 10 percent of the GNP.

On the surface, Bangladesh seems like a worthy recipient of foreign aid. It is an ideal testing ground for the new "basic needs" strategy so popular among major donors like the World Bank and AID. By meeting the basic needs of the poor—food, shelter, health care and education—the aid agencies hope to lay the groundwork for "growth with equity" instead of economic growth alone, which in the past has usually bypassed the poor. But unfortunately, it is far easier to talk about "basic needs" development programs than to implement them. Implementation is the responsibility of the recipient government, which is often more interested in meeting the not-so-basic needs of the rich and powerful than in helping the poor. As we discovered in Bangladesh, programs which on paper help the needy often look very different in the field.

Food Aid for the Elite

About one-quarter of the aid to Bangladesh comes in the form of food aid. The United States provides roughly one-third of this food aid under Titles I, II, and III of the Agricultural Trade Development and Assistance Act (Public Law 480). Under Title I, the Bangladesh government buys American food with concessionary loans and then distributes it according to its own policies. Title II food, given as a grant for disaster relief and humanitarian purposes, is usually disbursed through private voluntary agencies. Under the newly created Title III program, food will be provided to the government as under Title I, but the loan will be written off if the government uses the revenues from the sale of the food for development projects.

Since 1974, most American food aid has come to Bangladesh under the Title I program, giving the Bangladesh government virtually total control over food aid distribution. The Bangladesh government sells the Title I food at subsidized prices through its ration system. Ironically, most of the food aid goes to those who can best afford to pay the market price: the urban middle class. Twenty-seven percent of rationed food grains is allotted to members of the military, police and civil service, and to the employees of large enterprises; another 30 percent goes to the predominantly middle-class ration holders in the six urban areas. Nine percent is supplied to mills which sell flour to bakeries catering to the urban consumer.[2] It is no secret that the primary purpose of the ration system is to keep prices low for the politically volatile urban population.

The urban ration system is rife with corruption. A December 1977 AID memorandum reports: "The number of urban ration recipients appears now to equal or exceed the total urban population, a finding that would seem to suggest large-scale system leakages." As examples of these leakages, the document cites "double listing of recipients, padded rolls, black marketing of all types."[3]

Although 90 percent of Bangladesh's people live in the countryside, only one-third of the government's rationed foodgrains are allotted to rural areas. In theory, the ration of rural inhabitants is half that of city dwellers, but in practice they receive even less. The rural ration dealers siphon a substantial portion of the foodgrains and sell them on the black market. For this reason, a dealership is a key form of political patronage. The local dealer in Katni's area received the job because his father-in-law had been head of the local administrative body, the union council. As a result of "leakages," only an estimated 14 percent of the rural population receive any grain from the ration system.[4]

During our nine-month stay in Katni, the villagers were able to buy rationed foodgrains on only five occasions. Each time their quota was only one-half pound of grain per family member. As one villager remarked in disgust, "That is not enough for a single meal—it's hardly worth my time to go and buy it."

Although they recognize the shortcomings of the government's ration system, many aid donors insist that food aid has the beneficial effect of increasing the overall availability of foodgrains in Bangladesh. However, the main problem of the poor is not lack of supply, but lack of purchasing power. Even when rice was plentiful and selling at a reasonable price in the bazaar, the poor of our village went hungry. Title II foodgrains, distributed by voluntary agencies through food-for-work projects, sometimes provide temporary relief to the rural poor but in the long run as we have noted, these rural works projects primarily benefit the large landowners.

Food aid also has adverse long-term effects on agricultural development. Despite the stipulation in P.L. 480 that American food aid should relate to "efforts by aid-receiving countries to increase their own agricultural production," the U.S. Embassy in Dacca acknowledged in a 1976 cable that, "The incentive for Bangladesh government leaders to devote attention, resources, and talent to the problem of increasing domestic foodgrain production is reduced by the security provided by U.S. and other donors' food assistance."[5] Moreover, food aid undermines domestic food production by reducing the government's need to procure grain from local farmers and thus support prices at harvest time.

The new Title III "Food for Development" agreement with the Bangladesh government is designed to reduce these adverse consequences. Theoretically, government revenues from the sale of the 800,000 tons of American Title III wheat will be devoted to "self-help" rural development and health care projects. But this is little more than an accounting procedure, as money which would otherwise be allocated for these purposes will be released for other uses. As one experienced aid official told us, "Most of the money will probably end up being used to build new staff quarters for the military."

In fact, as this official explained, the main reformist thrust of Title III in Bangladesh lies not in the use of funds, but rather in policy changes tied to the agreement. Chief among these is the stipulation that the Bangladesh government must distribute at least half the wheat through open market sales to private traders. These sales are designed to keep prices from soaring beyond the reach of the poor in the lean season before the harvest—a tacit admission that food aid is more likely to reach the poor if sold on the open market than if distributed through the government's ration system. But whether or not the open market sales will succeed in holding down lean season prices is questionable. Prices soar primarily because of hoarding by merchants, so selling them more food may simply give them greater opportunities for profit. The World Bank notes that in order for open market sales to succeed, the government must "make no announcement as to the quantity available for this operation, thereby minimizing speculation by private dealers."[6] Given the cozy relationship between merchants and government officials, prospects do not seem bright.

Proponents of continued food aid to Bangladesh argue that even though the vast majority of food goes to feed the middle and upper classes, the poor would be worse off without it. Without food aid to supply the ration system, the rich would buy their rice on the market. If domestic foodgrain production falls short of the country's requirements, market prices would then soar beyond the reach of the poor. This dilemma leaves the rich of Bangladesh in a position to blackmail the donors: if you cut off our food aid, we won't be the ones to starve.

But the extent to which there is a shortfall between the country's production and its consumption needs is not clear. The sale of foodgrains through the ration system is a major source of government income, providing about one-fifth of the government revenue budget in fiscal year 1977. To ensure continuing food aid and revenue from its sale, the Bangladesh government is said by aid

"Ironically, most of the food aid goes to those who can best afford to pay the market price, the urban middle class."

officials to consistently underestimate the amount of each harvest in its reports to the international donors.[7] Today Bangladesh must produce about 15 million metric tons of foodgrains to feed its people.[8] Estimates of current production vary widely. The World Bank estimate for 1977-78 is 13.3 million metric tons,[9] but the FAO figure for 1977 is 19.6 million.[10] No one really knows, but Bangladesh might even now be self-sufficient in the production of foodgrains.

Notwithstanding various "self-help" provisions, food aid by its very nature can only address the symptoms of hunger, not its underlying causes. The logic is simple and compelling: if people are hungry, give them food. But instead of feeding needy people, food aid often strengthens the very forces which create hunger. In Bangladesh, food aid bolsters the elite and undermines any impulse towards self-reliance. In 1976, a U. S. Senate study recommended the phasing out of food aid to Bangladesh over a five-year period, following the advice of experts who believed that a commitment to terminate food aid "was the only way to force the government to take the necessary actions for eventual self-sufficiency."[11] This of course raises the question of why it should be necessary to "force" a government to act in the interests of its own people. This recommendation has not interrupted the flow of American food aid to Bangladesh.

Project Aid: A Tubewell for the Village Landlord

Aid to specific development projects would seem to offer donors greater scope for translating their concern for the poor into concrete action. Indeed, much project aid goes to the rural areas, where most of Bangladesh's needy people live. In their project descriptions, the donors frequently identify their "target group" as Bangladesh's small farmers. Unfortunately, most of their aid misses the mark.

Project aid reached Katni in the form of a deep tubewell for irrigation, one of 3000 installed in northwestern Bangladesh by a World Bank project. On paper, the tubewell will be used by a farmers' cooperative formed especially for the purpose. According to the press release which announced the project, each tubewell "will serve from 25 to 50 farmers in an irrigation group."[12] In reality, the tubewell in our village was the personal property of one man: Nafis, the biggest landlord of the area. The irrigation group, of which Nafis was supposedly the manager, was no more than a few signatures he had collected on a scrap of paper.

Nafis and his younger brothers inherited 70 acres of land from their father, who had become rich by serving as a rent collector and a procurer of village women for the local *zamindar* during the colonial era. While attending college, Nafis joined the late Sheikh Mujib's Awami League and soon became an influential figure in local politics. Shortly after independence he was appointed vice chairman of the union council, in which position he misappropriated the few blankets and sheets of corrugated tin which came to the village as postwar relief supplies.

The tubewell was by far Nafis's greatest patronage plum. Although each tubewell cost the donors and the government about U.S. $12,000, Nafis paid less than $300 for his, mostly in bribes to local officials. The tubewell sits in the middle of a 30-acre tract of Nafis's best land. Since it will yield enough water to irrigate twice that area, Nafis says the smaller farmers who till adjacent plots will be able to use his water—at a price. But the hourly rate he intends to charge is so high that few of his neighbors are interested. As a result his tubewell will not be used to its full capacity.

At first we were surprised that the beneficiary of the World Bank's aid should be the richest man in our village, but on closer inspection we learned that this was not so strange. A foreign expert working on the project told us, "I no longer ask who is getting the well. I know what the answer will be, and I don't want to hear it. One hundred percent of these wells are going to the big boys. Each *thana* (county) is allotted a certain number of tubewells. First priority goes to those with political clout: the judges, the magistrates, the members of parliament, the union chairmen. If any are left over, the local authorities auction them off. The rich landlords compete, and whoever offers the biggest bribe gets the tubewell. Around here the going price is 3000 *taka* (less than U.S. $200)."

"You see," he explained, "On paper, it's a different story. On paper, all the peasants know these tubewells are available. If they want to have one, they form themselves into a democratic cooperative, draw up a proposal and submit it to the union council, which judges the application on its merits. The union council then passes the proposal to the *Thana* Irrigation Team, which again judges the case on its merits. If the proposal is accepted, the foreign consultants verify that the site is technically sound. So on paper it all sounds quite nice. Here are the peasants organizing to avail themselves of this wonderful resource. When the high-level officials fly in from Washington for a three-day visit to Dacca, they look at these papers. They don't know what is happening out here in the field, and no one is going to tell them."

An evaluation sponsored by the Swedish International Development Authority (SIDA), which helped to finance the tubewell project, confirms that the experience of our village was typical. The evaluator concluded after examining 270 tubewells:

> It is not surprising that the tubewells have been situated on the land of the well-to-do farmers who are the chairmen and managers of the irrigation groups. It (would have) been more surprising if the tubewells had *not* been located on their land, with the existing rural power structure, maintained largely because of the unequal distribution of land.[13]

Given the social realities of rural Bangladesh, the outcome of the World Bank's tubewell project was entirely predictable.

For the poor of our village, the only conceivable benefit of the project will be the employment generated by Nafis's extra rice crop. Nafis plans to work part of his tubewell land with hired labor and to lease part to sharecroppers. (Since the yield on this irrigated land will be higher, Nafis intends to take two-thirds rather than his customary one-half of the crop: "After all," he says, "I bought the well.")

Against any employment benefits one must weigh the negative effects of the tubewell: with his extra income, Nafis will be better able to buy out smaller farmers when hard times befall them, driving them into the ever-growing ranks of the landless. He already has an eye on the plots nearest his tubewell.

What lessons has the World Bank learned from this project? One Bank official told us that the tubewell project "should not be used as an example of the Bank's current programs in Bangladesh," because it was conceived in 1969 before the Bank had adopted the basic needs strategy. But while new ideas may become fashionable among aid donors, the realities of rural Bangladesh remain the same. A look at the Bank's "Rural Development One" (RD-1) pilot project, launched in 1976, reveals the old contradictions present in the Bank's new directions.

New Directions?

RD-1 provides $16 million spread over seven of Bangladesh's 410 *thanas* for everything from rural works, credit and agricultural extension to the construction of government buildings. According to a Bank press release, "One of the most important goals of the project will be to reduce the domination of rural institutions by the more prosperous and politically influential farmers and to make farm credits and agricultural inputs (fertilizer, pumps, tubewells, insecticide and fuel) available to the 'small farmers' through the cooperative system."[14]

What has happened in reality? An unusually frank internal World Bank memorandum, evaluating the first year of RD-1, concludes that the implementation of the project is "unsatisfactory." The memo cites one cooperative as a typical example: "The manager (of the cooperative) owns 20 acres of land and has held his managerial position since inception, although he has been in jail for the past one and a half years . . . the TPO (Thana Project Officer) approved a loan of Tk/17,000 to this society in July/August 1977. Other members of this KSS (cooperative) were not aware of this loan. The TPO is unable to give any logical reason for approval of this credit."[15]

The memo also notes that the local project staff "appears to consider the filling out of innumerable forms to be its main function."[16] Because of widespread corruption and incompetence in the public works constructed under the project, roads were washing away and market buildings crumbling within months of their completion.

RD-1 has earned such notoriety in Bangladesh that even AID officials are quick to disassociate themselves from it. One AID official told us: "Don't assume our programs are like that. In our view, RD-1 is a project which has been captured by the rich." Nevertheless, in early 1979 Bank officials in Washington told us that the project is a success, and that they plan to launch a second project on the same lines in the near future.

Despite much talk of "targeting" assistance to the rural poor, AID's rural development projects face the same basic obstacle: the unequal distribution of land and power in rural Bangladesh means that large landowners will inevitably seize the lion's share of scarce aid-provided resources. One of AID's main activities in Bangladesh is the provision of fertilizer; in fact, the recent Title III food aid agreement specifies that over half the proceeds from the sale of the food will be used to purchase and distribute fertilizer.[17] Fertilizer prices are highly subsidized by the Bangladesh government, ostensibly to help small and large farmers alike to increase their production. But who does the subsidy really benefit? According to the World Bank: "By most accounts farmers usually have to pay the market rather than the subsidized price, the margin benefiting the middleman instead of the farmer."[18] The middlemen are the same merchants, landowners and local officials who hold the reins of power in rural Bangladesh. As usual, not much "trickles down" to the poor.

AID is also becoming involved with rural electrification, which is enjoying a new upsurge of popularity among aid donors in Bangladesh. According to one AID official, electrification will bring such tangible benefits as supplying power for tubewells, increasing the use of radio for agriculture extension services, spurring the growth of local industries, and, at last but not least, making government officials less reluctant to get out into the countryside.

Of all these ostensible benefits, the growth of rural industry would seem most likely to help the poor, who are desperately in need of employment. But what kind of industries are likely? In an interview with OXFAM-America, an experienced foreign field worker described how the Germans and Japanese are trying to market high technology rice mills in Bangladesh. Rather than generating employment, these mills would displace the labor of millions of poor rural women who earn their livelihood by manually processing rice. "It's generally true that expensive technology introduced into an unequal situation increases the inequality," the field worker explained. "The poorest people suffer most . . . In the present situation, large-scale electrification would lead to large numbers of high technology mills, resulting in the immediate unemployment of these women who would become destitute because there is no other alternative."[19]

Who Is to Blame?

Confronted with the failure of rural development aid to benefit the poor, foreign donors predictably blame the Bangladesh government, not themselves. "The Bank is not blind to these things," one World Bank official told us, "but our ability to do anything about them is limited. If the government doesn't have the will to help the small farmers, we can't force them to do it. We can advise, we can write provisions into our projects, but without that genuine commitment on the part of the government it just won't work."

But when we spoke to a high-ranking Bengali diplomat, he put it another way: "We have no control over these projects. The World Bank and the other international agencies tell us what to do, and we do it. If they want to give us tubewells or fertilizers because it's good for business in their countries, what are we to do? After all, they have the money."

Both arguments contain an element of truth. Drawing its support from the urban and rural elites, the Bangladesh government does lack the political will to help the poor. But aid donors design and finance projects which time and again benefit these same elites. In veiled statements in confidential documents, the donors occasionally criticize the government, but money speaks louder than words. Indeed, quantity rather then quality seems to be the prime concern of many international aid agencies. That there is a contradiction between self-reliance and the absorption of an ever growing volume of foreign aid seems to escape them.

Why do aid institutions push money on Bangladesh? Partly because aid is good for business back home. The U.S. Commerce Department's publication *Commerce America* reports happily: "In

---

"For Bangladesh's poor, the quiet violence of starvation and the less subtle violence of state repression are two sides of the same shiny foreign coin."

---

fiscal year 1977 AID commodity expenditures [worldwide] amounted to $771,132,000, 98 percent of which was in the U.S."[20] Moreover, foreign aid has spawned vast bureaucracies with a vested interest in their own survival and expansion.

But the main motives behind foreign aid are related to long-term political and economic interests. A prominent aid official wrote in 1964, before the basic needs rhetoric became fashionable:

> In the most general sense, the main objective of foreign assistance, as of many other tools of foreign policy, is to produce the kind of political and economic environment in the world in which the United States can best pursue its own social goals . . . The second objective, which concerns the immediate future, is internal stability, which is sought by giving politically popular types of aid to existing governments, by the prevention of internal disorders . . . The third major objective of foreign assistance is security of the United States and its allies from external aggression.[21]

In Bangladesh foreign aid helps to insure that the government will look kindly on foreign investors, whose eyes are above all on the country's vast reserves of natural gas.[22] It helps to promote "internal stability" by allowing the government to buy the support of the urban elite with subsidized food and government jobs, and the support of the rural elite with patronage given under the guise of rural development.

In its 1978 budget presentation to Congress, AID notes: "The U. S. political interests in Bangladesh are limited and reflect a concern for the impact that instability in Bangladesh could have on the subcontinent as a whole."[23] Bangladesh borders on the politically volatile Indian state of West Bengal and on hill areas where India has been fighting tribal insurgents for years. Recently Zbigniew Brzezinski, the National Security Advisor for the President of the

United States, has hinted at Bangladesh's strategic importance: "Today the area of crisis is a group of states on the shores of the Indian Ocean—literally an arc of instability, which can be drawn on a map from Chittagong in Bangladesh, through Islamabad, all the way to Aden. Their internal fragility, social and political, could interact with the projection of Soviet power . . . "[24]

But foreign development aid alone can not buy political "stability" in Bangladesh—it must be backed up by the force of arms. While food aid provides indirect financing for the government's repressive apparatus, military assistance directly bolsters forces which crush any challenge to the status quo. For Bangladesh's poor, the quiet violence of starvation and the less subtle violence of state repression are two sides of the same shiny foreign coin.

Arming the Status Quo

Early one morning as we rode on a bus north from Dacca, we passed a military cantonment. Through the heavy mist we saw a line of prisoners, their heads shaven and their arms chained, marching under armed guard near the road. The genial chatter in the bus stopped abruptly as the passengers absorbed the scene in silence. We had just caught a glimpse of the realities of political repression in Bangladesh.

The governments which have come and gone in Bangladesh have one thing in common: each has used force to suppress opposition. Sheikh Mujib, whose overwhelming victory in the 1970 elections precipitated the independence struggle, originally enjoyed tremendous popular support. But within two years disenchantment set in, as the corruption and incompetence of the ruling Awami League plunged the country into economic chaos. In response to growing opposition, Mujib declared a state of emergency in late 1974, suspending civil liberties and instituting press censorship. In January 1975, he scrapped the parliamentary system, outlawed all political parties except his own, and declared himself president. The prisons filled with his political opponents.

Mujib was assassinated in August 1975 by disgruntled junior army officers, paving the way for a series of coups. In November 1975, after a convulsive army mutiny, Major-General Ziaur "Zia" Rahman seized power as head of a new martial law regime. In July 1976, Zia's government hung Colonel Abu Taher, a hero of the independence war and leader of the November army mutiny, in Bangladesh's first official political execution since the days of British colonial rule. When a mutiny again broke out in the armed forces in October 1977, Zia responded with mass executions of hundreds of soldiers, setting yet another ominous precedent.

In its 1977 Annual Report, Amnesty International estimated that there were from 10,000 to 15,000 political prisoners in Bangladesh, most held without trial. Within the jails, the organization reported that treatment of prisoners "borders on conditions that are inhuman."[25] This dismal human rights situation soon began to

"Until Americans take a hard look at the political realities in countries like Bangladesh, they can expect their foreign aid dollars to perpetuate rather than alleviate poverty."

tarnish Zia's image in the West. In order to both appease critics abroad and legitimize his rule at home, Zia decided to gradually return Bangladesh to "democracy."

In June 1978, Zia ran for president in an election held under martial law, and won a predictable victory. Then in parliamentary elections held in February 1979, his party won a large majority of seats. However, only 40 percent of the electorate turned out to vote.[26] A senior Bangladesh army officer candidly revealed the motives behind the elections: "The West, and especially the U.S. Congress, likes it if we can be called a democracy," he told a foreign journalist. "It will make it easier for us to get aid. That is the main importance of the election."[27]

Zia himself echoed this view in a speech to foreign reporters: "Now, with this election and the democratic process being restored, more private investment should come into this country."[28]

Despite some improvements, the human rights situation in Bangladesh is still far from rosy. During Zia's five years in power, more than 1,000 military personnel are reported to have been executed. On May 30, 1981, the illusion of stability was shattered when Zia himself died in a hail of gunfire in an abortive coup attempt.[29]

The most serious human rights violations in Bangladesh today are in the southeastern Chittagong Hill Tracts, where the government is trying to crush a movement for limited autonomy. A statement by the tribal movement, the Shanti Bahini (Peace Army), published in a prominent Indian journal, charges that the Bangladesh army has unleashed a reign of terror, including rapes, summary executions, indiscriminate burnings and lootings of entire villages, and the creation of "strategic villages" which resemble concentration camps.[30] One of the few foreign journalists who managed to visit the area reported: "The only able-bodied young civilians I saw roped together, through the town bazaar at Kaptai, 30 miles east of Chittagong."[31]

Foreign aid dollars are directly supporting Bangladesh's military and police forces. The British government is providing U.S. $1.3 million worth of telecommunications equipment to the Bangladesh police, and eight British military officers are helping to establish a military staff college north of Dacca. Several foreign governments are providing financing for a road in the Chittagong Hill Tracts which will facilitate troop movements.[32]

The United States, for its part, is providing aid under the International Military Education and Training Program (IMET), which brings Bengali officers to the United States to study "management techniques." The State Department's rationale for the IMET program is "to improve an institution which contributes to stability in Bangladesh and in the region."[33] But the stability to be purchased by propping a regime which rules in favor of Bangladesh's narrow elite is likely to prove illusory.

In the long run, economic development is the key to political stability. But it does not follow that in the short run political stability is the key to economic development. This is especially true if what is stabilized is the political power of a narrow elite which puts its own interests above those of the country's poor majority. Until Americans take a hard look at the political realities in countries like Bangladesh, they can expect their foreign aid dollars to perpetuate rather than alleviate poverty.

Family Planning Comes to Bangladesh

Billboards along the riverside encourage Bangladeshis to limit the size of their families. *Photo by Benedict Tisa.*

"Overpopulation" is not the cause of poverty in Bangladesh. The country could easily feed its present population—and more—if the social constraints on agricultural production were removed. Even though population growth is not the main problem, many villagers want access to family planning.

As we learned in Katni, villagers have good reasons for wanting children. Children's labor is a vital part of the household economy, and parents rely on their sons to support them in their old age. Because the infant and child mortality rate is so high in Bangladesh, parents must have many children in order to ensure that at least one son will survive. But once villagers have enough children to meet their needs, they are often very interested in birth control. Women are tired of constant pregnancies, and parents realize that too many children can be a drain on the family's resources.

Soon after our arrival in Katni, we were bombarded with pleas for birth control pills. AID had already given millions of dollars worth of pills to the Bangladesh government to be distributed free of charge, but the only pills the village women had seen were marketed by a travelling merchant woman at a price of eight *taka*—more than the average daily wage—for a month's cycle. Several daring women had bought them without their husbands' knowledge, but lacking instructions on how to use the pills, they soon became pregnant.

In response to the villagers' pleas, we visited the government family planning office in the nearest town and requested that extension workers come to our village. After their arrival, we learned why the

demand for birth control in the villages was not being met. Wearing expensive jewelry and silk *saris,* the extension workers were educated, middle-class town women, separated from the village women by a gulf of arrogance and indifference. They addressed the villagers in upper-class Bengali and in their presence asked us how we could stand the "inconvenience" of living in a dirty village. After they left, the villagers inquired if they were our sisters from America.

The family planning workers promised to return within three days with a supply of pills, but it was many weeks before the villagers saw them again. They claimed that they could not come because their jeep had broken down, and they were unable to walk the five miles to the village from the town, a distance many villagers covered by foot every day. This explanation did not inspire confidence. Nor did the ensuing discussion. The extension workers told the village women it was immodest not to wear blouses beneath their *saris.* Unable to afford blouses, the village women sat for a moment in embarrassed silence.

Although the extension workers left behind a carton of pills, the villagers doubted they would ever return to replenish the stock, much less to supervise the women's taking of the pill. As one village woman told us, "All government officers care about is their salary. They sit in offices and drink tea. What do they care about us?"

Our village's encounter with the family planning service illustrates the failure of Bangladesh's health care system to reach the poor. Over three-fourths of Bangladesh's doctors serve the 10 percent of the people who live in urban centers; in the rural areas there is only one doctor for every 40,000 people.[1] The few health care workers employed in the countryside often share the attitude of the women who visited our village: they look down on the rural poor.

Although the aid donors are now recognizing the limitations of using upper-class government servants for family planning work in the villages, the alternatives they have developed may actually be making matters worse. AID has launched a "contraceptive inundation" program for birth control in Bangladesh. The countryside is literally being flooded with cheap birth control pills, distributed by undertrained field workers or sold through small village shops. In the words of Dr. Ravenholt, the head of AID's population program: "The principle involved in the household distribution of contraceptives can be demonstrated with Coca Cola . . . If one distributed an ample, free supply of Coca Cola into each household, would not poor illiterate peasants drink as much Coca Cola as the rich literate residents?"[2]

But as Stephen Minkin, the former head of UNICEF's nutrition program in Bangladesh, points out, birth control pills are a powerful drug, not a soft drink. Given without adequate supervision, they are potentially harmful to women and children. Pregnant women who take the pill increase the risk of cardiovascular birth defects in their children. Moreover, the use of the pill by nursing mothers may decrease their milk supply, contributing to infant malnutrition.[3]

In the absence of a health care system designed to meet the needs of the rural poor, aid for family planning, like aid for rural development, more often hurts than helps.

Photo by Hartmann/Boyce.

8. What Can We Do?

We as Americans *can* help to end the needless hunger in Bangladesh.

First, we can work to halt military and economic assistance which bolsters Bangladesh's narrow elite at the expense of the country's poor majority. Conventional wisdom suggests that we should give more aid to Bangladesh, not less. Many concerned Americans are dismayed at how little of our national wealth we devote to "helping the poor countries." But we must re-examine this charity impulse. We must look beyond the symptoms of hunger to the causes. In particular, we must ask whether the best way to help the poor is to give arms, money and food to the rich. Only the Bangladeshi people can carry out the social reconstruction which alone can bring an end to hunger in Bangladesh. But we, as Americans, have both the power and the responsibility to remove those obstacles which our government's "aid" places in their way.

Secondly, we can assist the many people in Bangladesh and throughout the third world who are working to mobilize the poor for development and social change. We can offer financial support to groups working in their own communities, using local organizers, and starting with the immediate needs of their people.

Thirdly, we can continue to educate ourselves and others about the needless hunger of millions of people throughout the world. No issue more clearly reveals the gap between technological possibilities and social realities, or points more vividly to the urgent need for social change. As we in the United States learn about the role of our political and economic institutions in perpetuating hunger, we will find that we must reshape our own society. Here, as in Bangladesh, we must work to ensure that the well-being of many is not sacrificed to the narrow interests of a few. In this struggle, the poor of Bangladesh are our allies.

Betsy Hartmann and James Boyce lived in Bangladesh in 1974–1976 on grants from Yale University. This book is based upon their experiences in the village of Katni where they lived for nine months. They are also the authors of *A Quiet Violence: A View from a Bangladesh Village* (Food First Books, 1983).

Betsy Hartmann is the author of *Reproductive Rights and Wrongs: The Global Politics of Popualtion Control and Contraceptive Choice* (Harper & Row, 1987).

James Boyce is the author of *Agrarian Impasse in Bengal: Institutional Constraints to Technological Change* (Oxford University Press, 1987), and currently Assistant Professor of Economics at the University of Massachusetts, Amherst.

Notes

1. The Paradox

1. Food and Agriculture Organization, Bangladesh: Country Development Brief, 1973, cited in *Food First*, p. 19.
2. World Bank, *Bangladesh: Development in a Rural Economy*, Volume 1: The Main Report, September 15, 1974, p. 1.
3. According to World Bank, *Bangladesh: Current Trends and Development Issues*, December 15, 1978, p. iv, per capita income is $91. Life expectancy from United States Agency for International Development (A. I. D.), *FY 1978, Submission to Congress: Asia Programs*, February, 1977, p. 16.
4. World Bank, *Bangladesh: Development in a Rural Economy*, Volume 1: The Main Report, September 15, 1974, p. 2.
5. *Nutrition Survey of Rural Bangladesh*, 1975-76, Institute of Nutrition and Food Science, University of Dacca, December, 1977.
6. World Bank, *Bangladesh: Current Trends and Development Issues*, December, 15, 1978, country data, p. 1.
7. "World Hunger, Health and Refugee Problems: Summary of Special Study Mission to Asia and the Middle East," report prepared for the Subcommittee on Labor and Public Welfare and the Subcommittee on Refugees and Escapees, Senate Committee on the Judiciary, January 1976, p. 99.
8. World Bank, *Bangladesh: Current Economic Situation and Development Policy Issues*, May 19, 1977, p. 34.
9. Rice yields for 1928-32 can be found in Nafis Ahmad, *An Economic Geography of East Pakistan*, London: Oxford University Press, 1968, p. 129.
10. *Ibid*, p. 75.

2. Riches to Rags

1. William Bolts, *Considerations on Indian Affairs*, London, 1772, cited in Ramkrishna Mukherjee, *The Rise and Fall of the East India Company*, New York: Monthly Review Press, 1974, pp. 302-303.
2. Helen Lamb, "The 'State' and Economic Development in India," in S. Kuznets et al, ed., *Economic Growth: Brazil, India, Japan*, Durham, N.C.: Duke University Press, 1955, p. 468.
3. Cited in Mukherjee, p. 304.
4. Cited in Mukherjee, pp. 337-338.
5. Abu Abdullah, "Land Reform and Agrarian Change in Bangladesh," *The Bangladesh Development Studies*, volume IV, no. 1, January 1976, p. 69.

6. Cited in A.R. Mallick, *British Policy and the Muslims in Bengal,* Dacca: 1961.
7. Lamb, p. 490.
8. For example, Home Minister Sir Herbert Risley frankly described the motives behind the 1905 partition of Bengal along religious lines: "Bengal united is a power. Bengal divided will pull in different ways. . . . One of our main objects is to split up and thereby weaken a solid body of opponents to our rule." Quoted in A. Tripathi, *The Extremist Challenge: India Between 1890 and 1910,* Calcutta: Orient Longmans, 1967, p. 95.

3. Who Owns the Land?

1. F. Tomasson Jannuzi and James T. Peach, *Report on the Hierarchy of Interests in Land in Bangladesh,* Washington, D.C.: Agency for International Development, September 1977, pp. xxi, 30.
3. Azizur Rahman Khan, "Poverty and Inequality in Rural Bangladesh," in *Poverty and Landlessness in Rural Asia,* Geneva: International Labor Organization, 1977, p. 142.
3. Jannuzi and Peach, p. 70.
4. Khan, p. 159.

4. Siphoning the Surplus

1. Jannuzi and Peach, pp. 41-42, 81.
2. *Ibid,* pp. 42-43.
3. Edward J. Clay, "Institutional Change and Agricultural Wages in Bangladesh," paper presented at Agricultural Development Council Seminar on Technology and Factor Markets, Singapore, August 9-10, 1976.

5. The Inefficiency of Inequality

1. "Bangladesh: Rural Development in four thanas in Kushtia District," Netherlands Ministry of Foreign Affairs, International Technical Assistance Department, February, 1978.
2. Jannuzi and Peach, pp. 43-44.
3. *Ibid.,* p. xxvii.
4. World Bank, *Bangladesh: Current Trends and Development Issues,* December 15, 1978, p. 3.
5. *Agricultural Employment in Bangladesh,* Government of Bangladesh—UNDP/FAO Mission, April 1977. Cited in "Agricultural Unemploy-

ment in Bangladesh, Prospects for the Next Decade," USAID/DACCA cable A-57, September 27, 1977.

6. USAID/DACCA cable A-57, September 27, 1977.
7. *Ibid.*
8. Jannuzi and Peach, p. 88.
9. World Bank, *Rural Development: Sector Policy Paper,* February 1975.
10. "Land Reform and Related Matters," cable from American Embassy, Dacca to Secretary of State, Washington, D.C., December 1977.
11. World Bank, *Bangladesh: Current Trends and Development Issues,* December 15, 1978, p. 32.
12. *Ibid.*, pp. 24, 29-30, 87.
13. *Ibid.*, p. 24.
14. *Ibid.*, p. 22.
15. *Ibid.*, p. 25.
16. *Ibid.*, p. 7.
17. *Ibid.*, p. 49.
18. James P. Sterba, "Bangladesh Losing Skilled Workers by Thousands," *New York Times,* March 11, 1979.

6. What Is the Alternative?

1. Figures based on data in Jannuzi and Peach.
2. Jannuzi and Peach, p. 87.
3. Rounaq Jahan, *Pakistan: Failure in National Integration,* Dacca: Oxford University Press and New York: Columbia University Press, 1973, pp. 18-19.
4. "A. I. D. Development Strategy for Bangladesh," USAID Mission to Bangladesh, January 1978, submitted to strategy meeting in Washington, D.C., February 6-7, 1978, p. 9.
5. See Premen Addy and Ibne Azad, "Politics and Culture in Bengal," *New Left Review,* no. 79, May-June 1973.
6. Kevin Rafferty, " 'Lucky' in Bangladesh," *The Washington Post,* September 3, 1978.
7. Jannuzi and Peach, p. 73.

7. Foreign Aid: A Helping Hand?

1. World Bank, *Bangladesh: Current Trends and Development Issues,* December 15, 1978, p. 18.

2. Figures on distribution through the ration system are based on information in World Bank, *Bangladesh: Food Policy Review*, December 12, 1977.

3. "Aspects of the Public Food Distribution System," AID/Dacca memorandum, December 1, 1977.

4. *Ibid.*

5. Cable cited in Donald McHenry and Kai Bird, "Food Bungle in Bangladesh," *Foreign Policy*, Summer 1977.

6. World Bank, *Bangladesh: Current Trends and Development Issues*, December 15, 1978, p. 35.

7. McHenry and Bird.

8. Calculated as follows: According to the 1978 World Bank report (p. 27), the Government of Bangladesh estimates the average daily foodgrain requirement at 15.5 ounces per capita; multiplied by the World Bank Bangladesh population estimate of 85 million, we get 13.66 million metric tons; adding 10 percent for seed, feed and wastage the figure comes to 15 million metric tons.

9. World Bank, *Bangladesh: Current Trends and Development Issues*, December 15, 1978, p. 2.

10. FAO, *Production Yearbook, 1977*, Rome, 1978.

11. "World Hunger, Health, and Refugee Problems: Summary of Special Study Mission to Asia and the Middle East," report prepared for the Subcommittee on Health, Committee on Labor and Public Welfare and the Subcommittee on Refugees and Escapees, Committee on the Judiciary, United States Senate, January 1976, p. 104.

12. International Development Association Press Release No. 70/38, July 1, 1970.

13. Per Arne Stroberg, "Water and Development: Organizational Aspects of a Tubewell Irrigation Project in Bangladesh," mimeo, Dacca, March 1977.

14. IDA Press Release No. 76/22, May 24, 1976.

15. World Bank Office Memorandum, Dacca, September 19, 1977, p. 5.

16. *Ibid.*, p. 3.

17. "Agreement Between the Government of the United States of America and the Government of the People's Republic of Bangladesh for a Public Law 480 Food for Development (Title III) Program," Annex B, August 1978, p. 5.

18. World Bank, *Bangladesh: Current Trends and Development Issues*, December 15, 1978, p. ii.

19. Michael Scott, *Aid to Bangladesh: For Better or Worse?* Oxfam-America/Institute for Food and Development Policy Impact Series No. 1, 1979, p. 10.

20. "AID Today—A Suppliers' View," *Commerce America*, September 11, 1978.

21. Hollis B. Chenery, "Objectives and Criteria for Foreign Assistance," in G. Rains, ed., *The United States and the Developing Economies*, New York: 1964, p. 81.

22. On the prospects of foreign investment in natural gas, see: N. M. J., "Murder in Dacca: Ziaur Rahman's Second Round," *Economic and Political Weekly* (Bombay), March 25, 1978. On the Bangladesh government's efforts to attract foreign investment, see James P. Sterba, "Bangladesh Wooing Businesses," *The New York Times*, April 9, 1979.

23. United States Agency for International Development, *FY 1978 Submission to the Congress: Asia Programs*, February 1977, p. 16.

24. "The World According to Brzezinski," Interview by James Reston, *The New York Times Magazine*, December 31, 1978.

25. Amnesty International, *Report of Amnesty International Mission to Bangladesh (4-12 April 1977)*, February 1978.

26. "Zia Party Set for Landslide in Polls," *The Guardian* (U. K.), February 19, 1979. See also: "Turnout Is Not Heavy In Bangladesh Voting for Parliament of 300," *The New York Times*, February 19, 1979.

27. S. Kamaluddin,"Bangladesh: Electing for Time to Think," *Far Eastern Economic Review*, January 12, 1979.

28. James P. Sterba, "Bangladesh Voters Support President," *New York Times*, Feb. 20, 1979.

29. Kai Bird, "The Unknown Zia," *The Nation* (New York), June 13, 1981.

30. "Revolt in Chittagong Hill Tracts," *Economic and Political Weekly*, Bombay, April 29, 1978.

31. Brian Eads, "Thousands Trapped in Bangladesh Terror," *The Observer* London, August 20, 1978.

32. Simon Winchester, "Where Britain may be aiding an armed dictatorship," *The Guardian* (London), December 20, 1977.

33. U.S. State Department, *Congressional Presentation, FY 1978*, Security Assistance Program, Volume I.

Family Planning Comes to Bangladesh

1. World Bank, *Bangladesh: Development in a Rural Economy*, Volume I, September 15, 1974, p. 197.

2. Stephen F. Minkin, "Abroad, the U. S. Pushes Contraceptives Like Coca Cola," *Los Angeles Times*, September 23, 1979.

3. *Ibid.*

Further Reading on Bangladesh

Abdullah, Abu, "Land Reform and Agrarian Change in Bangladesh," *Bangladesh Development Studies,* vol. IV, No. 1, January 1976.

Abdullah, A., M. Hossain and R. Nations, "Agrarian Structure and the IRDP — Preliminary Considerations," *Bangladesh Development Studies,* Vol. IV, No. 2, 1976.

Addy, Premen, and Ibne Azad, "Politics and Culture in Bengal," *New Left Review,* No. 79, May-June 1973.

Ahmad, Nafis, *An Economic Geography of East Pakistan,* London: Oxford University Press, 1968.

Ahmed, Feroz, "The Structural Matrix of the Struggle in Bangladesh," in Kathleen Gough and Hari Sharma, eds., *Imperialism and Revolution in South Asia,* New York: Monthly Review Press, 1973.

Alamgir, Mohiuddin, "Some Aspects of Bangladesh Agriculture: Review of Performance and Evaluation of Policies," *Bangladesh Development Studies,* vol. III, No. 3, July 1975.

Arens, Jenneki, and Jos van Beurden, *Jhagrapur: Poor Peasants and Women in a Village in Bangladesh,* Birmingham, England: Third World Publications, 1977.

Bertocci, Peter, "Elusive Villages: Social Structure and Community Organization in Rural East Pakistan," Unpublished Ph.D. thesis, Michigan State University, 1970.

Blair, Harry, "Rural Development, Class Structure and Bureaucracy in Bangladesh," *World Development,* vol. 6, no. 1, January 1978.

Bose, S. R. "The Comilla Cooperative Approach and the Prospects for Broad-based Green Revolution in Bangladesh," *World Development,* vol. 2, no. 8, August 1974.

Briscoe, John, "Politics of an International Health Programme," *Economic and Political Weekly* (Bombay), March 18, 1978.

Chowdhury, Anwarullah, *A Bangladesh Village: A Study of Social Stratification,* Dacca: Center for Social Studies, Dacca University, January 1978.

Clay, Edward, "Institutional Change and Agricultural Wages in Bangladesh," Dacca: Agricultural Development Council, mimeo, November 1976.

Clay, Edward, "Fool Aid and Food Policy in Bangladesh," *Food Policy,* vol. 4, no. 2, 1979.

Haq, M. Nurul, *Village Development in Bangladesh,* Comilla: Bangladesh Academy for Rural Development, 1973.

Haque, Wahidul, *et al.,* "Towards a Theory of Rural Development," *Development Dialogue* (Uppsala, Sweden), 1977: 2.

Hartmann, Betsy, and James Boyce, "Bangladesh: Aid to the Needy?" *International Policy Report,* Washington, D. C. : Center for International Policy, May 1978.

Huq, M. Ameerul, ed., *Exploitation and the Rural Poor,* Comilla: Bangladesh Academy for Rural Development, March 1976.

Islam, A. K. M. Aminul, *Victorious Victims: Political transformation in a traditional society,* Cambridge, Mass.: Schenkman Pub. Co., 1978.

Jahan, Rounaq, *Pakistan: Failure in National Integration,* New York: Columbia University Press, 1972.

Jannuzi, F. Tomasson, and James T. Peach, "Report on the Hierarchy of Interests in Land in Bangladesh," Washington, D. C. : United States Agency for International Development, September 1977.

Khan, Akhter Hameed, "A History of the Food Problem," Michigan State University Asian Studies Center, South Asia Series, Occasional Paper No. 20, reprinted by Agricultural Development Council, New York, October 1973.

Khan, Azizur Rahman, "Poverty and Inequality in Rural Bangladesh," in *Poverty and Landlessness in Rural Asia,* Geneva: International Labor Organization, 1977.

Khan, Azizur Rahman, "The Comilla Model and the Integrated Rural Development Program in Bangladesh," *World Development,* vol. 7, no. 4/5, April-May 1979.

Kinley, David, and Joseph Collins, "Rural Advances in Bangladesh," *Food Monitor,* no. 4, May-June 1978.

Lappé Frances Moore, and Joseph Collins, *Food First: Beyond the Myth of Scarcity,* Boston: Houghton Mifflin, 1977, New York: Ballantine Books, 1979.

Lifschultz, Lawrence, "Bangladesh: A State of Seige," *Far Eastern Economics Review,* August 30, 1974.

Lifschultz, Lawrence, *Bangladesh: The Unfinished Revolution,* London, Zed Press, 1979.

Maniruzzaman, T. , "Radical Politics and the Emergence of Bangladesh," in P. Brass and M. Franda, eds., *Radical Politics in South Asia,* Cambridge, Mass.: M. I. T. Press, 1974.

Maniruzzaman, T. , "Bangladesh: An Unfinished Revolution?" *Journal of Asian Studies,* vol. 34, no. 4, August 1975.

McHenry, Donald, and Kai Bird, "Food Bungle in Bangladesh," *Foreign Policy,* no. 27, Summer 1977.

Mukherjee, Ramkrishna, "The Social Background of Bangladesh," in K. Gough and H. Sharma, eds., *Imperialism and Revolution in South Asia,* New York: Monthly Review Press, 1973.

Mukherjee, Ramkrishna, *The Rise and Fall of the East India Company,* New York: Monthly Review Press, 1974.

Nations, Richard, "The Economic Structure of Pakistan: Class and Colony," *New Left Review* No. 68, July-August 1971.

Scott, Michael, *Aid to Bangladesh: For Better or Worse,* Oxfam-America/Institute for Food and Development Policy Impact Series, no. 1, 1979.

Stepanek, Joseph, *Bangladesh—Equitable Growth?* New York: Pergamon Press, 1979.

Stevens, Robert D., Hamza Alavi and Peter I. Bertocci, *Rural Development in Bangladesh and Pakistan,* Honolulu: University Press of Hawaii, 1976.

Van Schendel, Willem, "At Bay: The Peasantry of Bangladesh," Thesis, University of Amsterdam, 1974.

MORE BOOKS FROM FOOD FIRST

Shafted: Free Trade and America's Working Poor

EDITED BY CHRISTINE AHN
FOREWORD BY DENNIS KUCINICH
INTRODUCTION BY ANURADHA MITTAL

Fifteen working peoples' leaders—family farmers and farmworkers, fishermen and seamstresses—tell in their own words what the free trade regime has meant to them and their families and communities. Their wrenching and articulate accounts are supported by the analysis of four experts from the nonprofit, union, state government, and academic sectors. PAPERBACK, $10.00

To Inherit the Earth: The Landless Movement and the Struggle for a New Brazil

ANGUS WRIGHT AND WENDY WOLFORD

A groundbreaking study of Brazil's MST, or Landless Workers' Movement—one of the most important grassroots social movements in the world. Hundreds of thousands of poor, landless, and jobless women and men have, through their own nonviolent efforts, secured rights to millions of acres of farmland and are feeding themselves and their families and living with dignity. PAPERBACK, $15.95

Benedita da Silva: An Afro-Brazilian Woman's Story of Politics and Love

AS TOLD TO MEDEA BENJAMIN AND MAISA MENDONÇA
FOREWORD BY JESSE JACKSON

In this engaging memoir, Brazilian politician Benedita da Silva shares the inspiring story of her life as an advocate for the rights of women, people of color and the poor, and argues persuasively for economic and social human rights in Brazil and everywhere. PAPERBACK, $15.95

earthsummit.biz: The Corporate Takeover of Sustainable Development

KENNY BRUNO AND JOSHUA KARLINER

Transnational corporations have co-opted the rhetoric of social and environmental responsibility while avoiding actual responsibility for their actions. *earthsummit.biz* contains 18 muckraking case studies of the ways corporate behavior contradicts corporate PR, from Royal Dutch Shell to Monsanto to Phillip Morris. PAPERBACK, $12.95

Sustainable Agriculture and Resistance:
Transforming Food Production in Cuba
EDITED BY FERNANDO FUNES, LUIS GARCÍA, MARTIN BOURQUE, NILDA PÉREZ, AND PETER ROSSET

Sustainable agriculture, organic farming, urban gardens, smaller farms, animal traction, and biological pest control are all part of the new Cuban agriculture. In this book, Cuban authors offer details—for the first time in English—of these remarkable achievements. PAPERBACK, $18.95

Breakfast of Biodiversity:
The Truth about Rain Forest Destruction
JOHN VANDERMEER AND IVETTE PERFECTO
FOREWORD BY VANDANA SHIVA

Why biodiversity is in such jeopardy around the world and what steps must be taken to slow the ravaging of the rain forests. PAPERBACK, $16.95

The Future in the Balance:
Essays on Globalization and Resistance
WALDEN BELLO
EDITED WITH A PREFACE BY ANURADHA MITTAL

A new collection of essays by Third World activist and scholar Walden Bello on the myths of development as prescribed by the World Trade Organization and other institutions, and the possibility of another world based on fairness and justice. PAPERBACK, $13.95

Views from the South:
The Effects of Globalization and the WTO on Third World Countries
FOREWORD BY JERRY MANDER
AFTERWORD BY ANURADHA MITTAL
EDITED BY SARAH ANDERSON

This rare collection of essays by Third World activists and scholars describes in pointed detail the effects of the WTO and other Bretton Woods institutions. PAPERBACK, $12.95

Basta!

Land and the Zapatista Rebellion in Chiapas

REVISED EDITION

GEORGE A. COLLIER WITH ELIZABETH LOWERY QUARATIELLO

FOREWORD BY PETER ROSSET

The classic on the Zapatistas in a new revised edition, including a preface by Roldolfo Stavenhagen, a new epilogue about the present challenges to the indigenous movement in Chiapas, and an updated bibliography. PAPERBACK, $14.95

America Needs Human Rights

EDITED BY ANURADHA MITTAL AND PETER ROSSET

This new anthology includes writings on understanding human rights, poverty in America, and welfare reform and human rights. PAPERBACK, $13.95

The Paradox of Plenty: Hunger in a Bountiful World

Excerpts from Food First's best writings on world hunger and what we can do to change it. PAPERBACK, $18.95

A Siamese Tragedy: Development and Disintegration in Modern Thailand

WALDEN BELLO, SHEA CUNNINGHAM, AND LI KHENG POH

Critiques the failing economic system that has propelled the Thai people down an unstable path. PAPERBACK, $19.95

Dark Victory: The United States and Global Poverty

WALDEN BELLO, WITH SHEA CUNNINGHAM AND BILL RAU

FOREWORD BY SUSAN GEORGE

SECOND EDITION, WITH A NEW EPILOGUE BY THE AUTHOR

Offers an understanding of why poverty has deepened in many countries, and analyzes the impact of US economic policies. PAPERBACK, $14.95

Education for Action:
Graduate Studies with a Focus on Social Change
FOURTH EDITION
EDITED BY JOAN POWELL

A newly updated authoritative and easy-to-use guidebook that provides information on progressive programs in a wide variety of field. PAPERBACK, $12.95

Alternatives to the Peace Corps:
A Directory of Third World and US Volunteer Opportunities
TENTH EDITION
EDITED BY JENNIFER SAGE WILLSEA

Over one hundred listings of organizations in the United States and the Third World provide the prospective volunteer an array of choices to make their commitment count. PAPERBACK, $10.95

Call our distributor to place book orders. All orders must be prepaid. Client Distribution Services (800) 343-4499.

About Food First

(INSTITUTE FOR FOOD AND DEVELOPMENT POLICY)

Food First, also known as the Institute for Food and Development Policy, is a nonprofit research and education-for-action center dedicated to investigating and exposing the root causes of hunger in a world of plenty. It was founded in 1975 by Frances Moore Lappé, author of the bestseller *Diet for a Small Planet*, and food policy analyst Dr. Joseph Collins. Food First research has revealed that hunger is created by concentrated economic and political power, not by scarcity. Resources and decision-making are in the hands of a wealthy few, depriving the majority of land, jobs, and therefore food.

Hailed by *The New York Times* as "one of the most established food think tanks in the country," Food First has grown to profoundly shape the debate about hunger and development.

But Food First is more than a think tank. Through books, reports, videos, media appearances, and speaking engagements, Food First experts not only reveal the often hidden roots of hunger, they show how individuals can get involved in bringing an end to the problem. Food First inspires action by bringing to light the courageous efforts of people around the world who are creating farming and food systems that truly meet people's needs.

How To Become a Member or Intern of Food First

BECOME A MEMBER OF FOOD FIRST

Private contributions and membership gifts form the financial base of Food First/Institute for Food and Development Policy. The success of the Institute's programs depends not only on its dedicated volunteers and staff, but on financial activists as well. Each member strengthens Food First's efforts to change a hungry world. We invite you to join Food First. As a member you will receive a twenty percent discount on all Food First books. You will also receive our quarterly publication, *Food First News and Views*, and timely *Backgrounders* that provide information and suggestions for action on current food and hunger crises in the United States and around the world. If you want so subscribe to our internet newsletter, *Food Rights Watch*, send us an e-mail at foodfirst@foodfirst.org. All contributions are tax-deductible.

BECOME AN INTERN FOR FOOD FIRST

There are opportunities for interns in research, advocacy, campaigning, publishing, computers, media, and publicity at Food First. Our interns come from around the world. They are a vital part of our organization and make our work possible.

To become a member or apply to become an intern, just call, visit our web site, or clip and return the attached coupon to

Food First/Institute for Food and Development Policy
398 60th Street, Oakland, CA 94618, USA
Phone: (510) 654-4400 Fax: (510) 654-4551
E-mail: foodfirst@foodfirst.org
Web site: www.foodfirst.org

You are also invited to give a gift membership to others interested in the fight to end hunger.

JOINING FOOD FIRST

☐ I want to join Food First and receive a 20% discount on this and all subsequent orders. Enclosed is my tax-deductible contribution of:

☐ $100 ☐ $50 ☐ $35

NAME ______________________________

ADDRESS ______________________________

CITY/STATE/ZIP ______________________________

DAYTIME PHONE (______) ______________________________

E-MAIL ______________________________

ORDERING FOOD FIRST MATERIALS

ITEM DESCRIPTION	QTY	UNIT COST	TOTAL

PAYMENT METHOD:

☐ CHECK

☐ MONEY ORDER

☐ MASTERCARD

☐ VISA

MEMBER DISCOUNT, 20% $ ________

CA RESIDENTS SALES TAX 8.25% $ ________

SUBTOTAL $ ________

POSTAGE: 15% UPS: 20% ($2 MIN.) $ ________

MEMBERSHIP(S) $ ________

ADDITIONAL CONTRIBUTION $ ________

TOTAL ENCLOSED $ ________

____
NAME ON CARD

____
CARD NUMBER EXP. DATE

____
SIGNATURE

MAKE CHECK OR MONEY ORDER PAYABLE TO:

Food First, 398 - 60th Street, Oakland, CA 94618

FOR GIFT MEMBERSHIPS & MAILINGS, PLEASE SEE COUPON ON REVERSE SIDE

FOOD FIRST GIFT BOOKS

Please send a Gift Book to (order form on reverse side):

NAME ______________________________

ADDRESS ______________________________

CITY/STATE/ZIP ______________________________

FROM: ______________________________

FOOD FIRST PUBLICATIONS CATALOGS

Please send a Publications Catalog to:

NAME ______________________________

ADDRESS ______________________________

CITY/STATE/ZIP ______________________________

NAME ______________________________

ADDRESS ______________________________

CITY/STATE/ZIP ______________________________

NAME ______________________________

ADDRESS ______________________________

CITY/STATE/ZIP ______________________________

FOOD FIRST GIFT MEMBERSHIPS

❐ Enclosed is my tax-deductible contribution of:

❐ $100 ❐ $50 ❐ $35

Please send a Food First membership to:

NAME ______________________________

ADDRESS ______________________________

CITY/STATE/ZIP ______________________________

FROM: ______________________________